NEW BEGINNINGS
Breaking through to Unity

EARLY YEARS IN
LIVINGSTON'S
ECUMENICAL PARISH

James Maitland

SAINT ANDREW PRESS
EDINBURGH

First published in 1998 by
SAINT ANDREW PRESS
121 George Street, Edinburgh EH2 4YN

Copyright © James Maitland 1998

ISBN 0 7152 0755 5

British Library Cataloguing in Publication Data
A catalogue record for this book
is available from the British Library.

ISBN 0715207555

The publisher gratefully acknowledges
the financial assistance of The Drummond Trust.

Cover by Mark Blackadder.
Cover photograph of Revd James Maitland (foreground); and the Induction of the James Maitland and the Revd Brian Hardy at Midcalder, 6 January 1966 (© *photo:* Church of Scotland).
Printed and **bound** by Athenaeum Press Ltd, Gateshead, Tyne & Wear.

Photos on the last page of the art section
(top left and middle) are used by kind permission
of the *Linlithgowshire Journal & Gazette*.

CONTENTS

✳

DEDICATION

✳

For Elizabeth, Roslin, Barbara and Fiona

who did so much
to help one slow learner realise
that the joy of the Lord
is the only strength worth having …

ACKNOWLEDGMENTS

✳

by James Maitland

THIS book bears the name of one author, but in reality hundreds, literally hundreds, of people have had a big hand in it. Some of their names appear in print, but many many more have contributed in all kinds of ways to the work and I should like their quite indispensable contribution to be sincerely and thankfully acknowledged. Like so many in the Gospel story itself, the nameless ones in Livingston are the very stuff of the Spirit's working.

I am grateful to David Robertson, lately of Polbeth–Harwood Parish, West Lothian, for reading the script and making very helpful suggestions.

That George Mackay Brown has written such a moving commendation of the book in his Foreword is heartening for everyone involved in any way at all in reaching out towards that unity of the Lord's people for which he himself prayed: 'That they all may be one … that the world might believe.'

Special thanks must go to my wife Elizabeth, not only for doing the word-processing, but for so patiently managing to make sense of writing often hard to decipher and sometimes harder still to understand. I am also grateful to Cathy Arnot who did the typing of several 'try-out' sections, as well as the first chapter of the book.

FOREWORD

✳

by George Mackay Brown

WHEN I was a small boy in Stromness, Orkney, there were three Presbyterian kirks serving about 1700 people. I often used to pause and wonder about that, in the intervals of playing football and reading 'The Wizard'.

There was also a small 'piskey' church.

There were only two Catholics among us – an Irish barber called Paddy Mee and an Italian ice-cream man called Guilio Faggacia.

There was never the slightest religious intolerance, that I remember. There was just the slightest unease, among certain townsfolk, at the fact that there were three Presbyterian congregations: the Old Kirk, the UP Kirk and the Free Kirk. Despite the unions of 1900 and 1929, there was a certain stubborn pride in the sacrifice and labour that had gone into the buildings, and the bells and the organs, and all the history connected with kirks and manses and pastors.

Now all three congregations are gathered under one roof, and all resentments are forgotten.

Never, in my childhood, would the Catholic priest from Kirkwall have been invited to speak at a Kirk gathering. But such comings together are fairly frequent nowadays.

There was one faint movement towards ecumenism in my childhood. On Armistice Sunday a white-gowned figure appeared in the pulpit with the three dark-gowned ministers. This was Mr Thomson, the episcopal rector.

But I doubt whether the Catholic priest, in Kirkwall 15 miles away, was invited, even on such occasions.

It is a scandal that the seamless garment should be rent. But the work of invisible mending is now far advanced – as Jim Maitland shows in his valuable book – and the thread that makes whole what has been sundered will be very precious in the finished garment.

ABOUT THE AUTHOR

✳

by the Revd Professor J. McIntyre

WITH the advantage of hindsight, we can now see that certain distinguishing features characterised the ministry of one of the most visionary and accomplished ministers of the Church of Scotland in the second half of the twentieth century – the Revd Dr James Maitland.

His preaching, for example, was unique, combining profound religious fervour and logical persuasiveness, exegetical perception and theological content, rounded off with a rare capacity for apt literary quotation. He did not shirk difficult doctrinal or socio-economic subjects, tackling them on radio and television, or in addresses to mixed groups.

Running through all his preaching, speaking and thinking was a profound concern for the underprivileged – whether in Korea, Africa or Glasgow – for those depressed by what he once called 'soul-less industrialism'; and for those people in the 1950s suffering from tuberculosis, an affliction again threatening to return to our society. For him, his faith, his theology, his preaching earthed themselves in his conviction that Christian men and women had a God-given duty to become involved in the social, economic and political issues of their time.

But all these strands of interest and ability were woven together and strengthened by another of his passions – his commitment to Church unity, in particular the so-called 'Livingston Ecumenical Experiment'.

From its beginning with Dr Maitland and the Revd Brian Hardy of the Scottish Episcopal Church, the Experiment branched out to include Methodists and Congregationalists, with the Roman Catholic representatives co-operating at various levels.

Though he would have been the first to deny it, the success of that Experiment has to be attributed to the leadership and inspiration of James Maitland, and especially to his pastoral touch, his caring for people, and his ability to encourage the Churches to set up the Forum for the improvement of housing conditions, reallocation of houses and local educational arrangements.

So, if the parish is no longer called 'The Livingston Ecumenical Experiment', but 'The Livingston Ecumenical Parish', then the change is due to the fact that, for James, it was never an 'experiment' in the first place – but always the *real* thing.

✳

James Maitland

was born and brought up in the West Highlands of Scotland, received his schooling there, and from there went to Edinburgh University in 1934.

After graduating in Arts and Divinity he held parishes in Kirkcaldy, Edinburgh and Airdrie.

Between the Edinburgh and Airdrie charges he did a four years' stint as Warden of Community House in Glasgow, the mainland headquarters of the Iona Community.

He was appointed in 1966 as the first Church of Scotland minister to what was then called the Livingston Ecumenical Experiment, in which he worked as a member of the Team Ministry until his retirement from full time ministry in 1983.

In 1969 Edinburgh University conferred on him the honorary degree of Doctor of Divinity.

James Maitland died on 20th August 1996.

PART ONE
Finding One Another

*We had to celebrate and be glad
because this your brother was lost to you
and is now found.*

Luke 15: 32
(New International Version)

CHAPTER 1

Background to Livingston

BEFORE first light last Easter morning, you could have seen people in twos and threes straggling in from different parts of the new town of Livingston, making their way to the top of Dechmont Law, a little hill rising above the town at its northern end. By 6.30 am there were around one hundred Catholics, Baptists, Church of Scotland people and all the others singing powerfully, if not particularly tunefully, *'Thine be the glory, risen, conquering Son'* ... – and answering the call, *'Christ is risen' ...,* with the cry, *'He is risen indeed!'* Then, quite informally, a loaf was broken and the bread shared with everyone willing to take it.

If the Church is event before it is institution or organisation, if the Church is 'meeting Easter in people', then here was the Church at least in embryo, as God wants it, as God can make it, in and for Livingston, in and for every parish throughout the land.

I have always found it of particular significance at this Dawn Service on Easter Day that, in the view towards the east, the most eye-catching feature is Arthur's Seat and the city of Edinburgh, Scotland's capital. It was in Edinburgh in 1910 that the ecumenical movement as we know it was born, and born at a world conference not of bishops, moderators, elders, but of overseas missionaries from all the main Protestant denominations. The message of that conference was to ring round the Christian world for years to come, unmistakable in its simplicity and challenge: 'Only a united Church can be a missionary Church. Only a united Church can be a *Christian* Church.'

It was at this Conference that a young Christian, Azariah from Dornakal, was to plead for a fresh understanding of both Gospel and Church:

Through all the ages to come, the Indian Church will rise up in gratitude

*to attest the heroism and self-denying labours of the missionary body.
You have given your goods to feed the poor. You have given your bodies
to be burned. We ask also for love. Give us friends.*

A Church that is itself divided into separate and sometimes
actively hostile denominations cannot answer that plea. To offer
love and friendship in the name of Christ requires that love and
friendship become controlling realities throughout the life of
the entire body. Without this we are no better than the people
who so frustrated God's work in Christ.

*Woe to you, Scribes and Pharisees, hypocrites! – woe to you scholars
and leaders of the Churches – you say all the right things but your life
is in flagrant contradiction.* ~ (RSV) ~

For as a finale to that scene of warning plea after warning plea, and
in the Temple at that, Matthew portrays Jesus as crying out:

*O Jerusalem, Jerusalem, you who kill the prophets and stone those sent
to you, how often I have longed to gather your children together as a
hen gathers her chicks under her wings but you would not let me.
Look, look! there is your temple – forsaken by God.*
~ Matthew 23: 37,38 (NIV) ~

If this means anything, it surely means that to refuse to come together
in Christ's name and at his behest is tantamount to driving God
out from our temples, churches, cathedrals.

The ferment created by the Edinburgh Missionary Conference
deeply affected some of the ablest men and women in the Scottish
Churches. Some of them became outstanding protagonists of unity,
spreading the word by their writing, preaching and lecturing.
Amongst them were people like John and Donald Baillie, two of
the most influential theological thinkers of this century.

I can remember being taken by a remark made in passing by
John Baillie some time after his year as Moderator of the General
Assembly of the Church of Scotland. It was to the effect that the
World Church had come to have such reality for him that 'it means
more to me now than even my own dear Scottish Kirk'.

The students who sat under one or other of the Baillies, people who read their books, people who met them personally, could hardly avoid realising that to think seriously about the Gospel, to respond positively to its calling, raises radical questions demanding radical answers on our relationships personal, social, denominational.

Others were powerfully pleading the same cause. In Scotland people like Archie Craig, the first Secretary of the British Council of Churches, and Isobel Forrester of St Andrews, were well known throughout the Church as 'Apostles of unity'. In England William Temple, who has been described as 'the greatest Christian thinker since Augustine', and George K. Bell who took such a courageous and solitary stand in the House of Lords against the Government's policy of obliteration bombing towards the end of the Second World War, were outstanding in the whole-heartedness with which they championed the cause of reconciliation within the Church and through the Church.

In Germany Dietrich Bonhoeffer did much for the ecumenical movement during his life, and still more by his imprisonment and death at the hands of the Nazis. In his *Letters and Papers from Prison,* first published in this country just after the end of the War (SCM Press, 1953), he has a poem that perhaps as much as anything he ever wrote gives the measure of the man and his Christian greatness. Here are two verses:

Men go to God when he is sore bestead,
Find him poor and scorned, without shelter or bread,
Whelmed under weight of the wicked, the weak, the dead;
Christians stand by God in his hour of grieving.

God goes to every man when sore bestead,
Feeds body and spirit with his bread;
For Christians, pagans alike he hangs dead,
And both alike forgiving.

In France Abbé Couturier, who had suffered in the First World War and felt in his soul, as few others have done, the shame and pain of Church division, was responsible for starting the Week of Prayer for Christian Unity that is still observed throughout the

Church worldwide every January from 18th to 25th. Couturier used to say: 'Pray, pray. Go on praying and the Miracle will happen.'

As well as outstanding individuals whose word and influence helped prepare the way for a better obedience to the ecumenical vision, certain movements contributed as well. The Iona Community is one. Part of George MacLeod's prophetic achievement lay in the way he was able to lead people to find fresh understanding and inspiration in the spirituality and ways of working of the Columban Church, a Church that, whatever its differences from Roman outlook and practice, never for a moment thought of itself as anything but part and parcel of God's one Church.

'O God thou art the Father/Of all that have believed' is the opening of the best known of Columba's hymns, an original copy of which he is said to have sent to the Pope in Rome.

Part of George MacLeod's greatest boast in the Lord throughout the years was the clause in the Abbey's deed of trust that every Christian communion, Catholic, Orthodox, Protestant, must be allowed to celebrate its own rite in its own way within the Abbey Church. He saw, and helped many to see, that the renewal for which the Iona Community looks, prays and struggles, has to do with renewal of fellowship in the Spirit. To be in fellowship is healing and wholeness. To be out of fellowship is death.

A very telling expression of that Gospel truth can be seen in the way people who have shared the communion in the Sunday morning service in the Abbey church are encouraged immediately afterwards to move around in the cloisters 'breaking bread' with one another, particularly with those they have never met before. The bread used here is taken from the loaf baked in the Abbey kitchen, brought in at the 'great entrance' and laid on the holy table with the bread and wine of the Sacrament and thus made a telling symbol of how all our everyday living and relationships are meant to be affected by our sacramental sharing of the Lord's body and blood.

Jesus said – Jesus *says* – 'Come to me all who labour and are heavy laden.' What a nonsense we make of him and his word when we add on our 'closed shop' conditions and regulations!

The Tell Scotland movement, started by Tom Allan (Church of Scotland minister, friend and active partner of Billy Graham) and Ronnie Falconer (in charge of Scottish religious broadcasting with the BBC), made its own positive contribution to the breaking down of denominational barriers throughout the country. As the movement gathered momentum, others – such as Colin Day of the Iona Community, and Robert Mackie just returned to Scotland from a lifetime's ministry with the World Council of Churches – helped to give a still greater ecumenical emphasis to the work.

This was particularly evident in the annual week-long gatherings of people from all the Protestant denominations held in places like Dundee and Ayr. Participants learned so much and gave so much in the different 'workshops' about mission in their own localities; but perhaps the most important lesson of the whole experience was not just the sheer irrelevance of our denominational difference to 99 per cent of our concerns, but the positive value of being together and of realising that we have far, far more to bring us and hold us together than we can ever have to keep us apart. Just to catch a breath of the spirit of this kind of fellowship is to be left feeling uneasy and dissatisfied with a churchmanship whose distinctive *raison d'être* is still being sought in its exclusiveness. The Gospel we were rediscovering together is the very antithesis of exclusiveness. It is about new relationships with the poor, the forgotten, the despised, with those who frighten us, threaten us and treat us as enemies. To begin to tell this kind of Gospel to Scotland means first of all allowing ourselves as members of Christ's body to be brought into real and loving relationships with one another.

Two events – one overseas, the other here in Scotland – made more than a passing impression on the mind of many Church people in Scotland.

In 1947 the United Church of South India came into being. The bodies thus united were Anglican, Presbyterian, Congregational and Methodist – four of the mainstream Protestant Churches here in Scotland, and the very four that were to come together some twenty years later in the Livingston Ecumenical Experiment.

It added greatly to the appeal and challenge of this union in India that one of its chief architects and negotiators was a Church of Scotland missionary, Lesslie Newbigin, a man who had a worldwide reputation for the freshness, insightfulness and Gospel-centred forthrightness of his theological thinking. Dr Newbigin's writings (for example, *The Household of God,* published in 1952), as well as his addresses to General Assembly and other bodies during his furlough periods, did much to stimulate serious ecumenical enquiry amongst men and women of the Scottish Churches. That he was made one of the first bishops in the United Church of South India served as a personal and very telling reminder to his fellow Presbyterians in Scotland and elsewhere that the re-making of God's Church for his work of mission in the world of the twentieth and twenty-first centuries cannot be undertaken without a willingness to face changes of a quite radical and disturbing nature. These changes in Scotland may be very different from those in South India, but they will lose nothing of their costliness. Ecumenism on the cheap is, like cheap grace itself, an enemy of the Gospel.

The other event was the opening in Dunblane in 1962 of Scottish Churches House and the appointment of its first Warden, Ian Fraser, a Church of Scotland minister and member of the Iona Community.

The fact that seven denominations were prepared to put substantial money into a venture of this kind showed that complacent acceptance of denominationalism was being dented and that there was a belief, at least in embryo, that if the Gospel was to be allowed to have positive influence in shaping the future for Scotland's life and people, then the trustees of that Gospel would have to find more effective ways of engaging one another in the thinking, praying and common action that are both a condition and a consequence of hearing what the Spirit is saying to the Churches. Ian Fraser, and those working with him, did something much more important and much harder to do than organise conferences, workshops, training weekends, quiet days and retreats. People coming to the house for these and other reasons found themselves breathing a different air with something in it of a spiritual springtime. This, in my opinion, did more than anything else to begin the breakdown of that 'aggressive negativity' said to be Scotland's worst characteristic and never very far from the surface in great areas of Protestant Church life.

The World Council of Churches might not have had much direct influence on the ordinary membership of the Scottish Churches, but through its five-yearly Assemblies in different parts of the world, and through publications like *The Ecumenical Review*, it succeeded in keeping the claims of the ecumenical movement before a significant minority in all the mainstream Churches.

Part of the message of the first Assembly held at Amsterdam in 1948 was this:'Christ has made us his own and He is not divided. In seeking him we find one another.'

It was the Amsterdam Report that declared:

We have to remind ourselves and all men and women that God has put down the mighty from their seats and exalted the humble and meek. We have to learn afresh together to speak boldly in Christ's name both to those in power and to the people, to oppose terror, cruelty and race discrimination, to stand by the outcast, the prisoner and the refugee. We have to make of the Church in every place a voice for those who have no voice and a home where everyone will be at home. We have to learn afresh together what is the duty of the Christian man or woman in industry, in agriculture, in politics, in the professions and in the home. We have to ask God to teach us together to say 'No' and to say 'Yes' in truth. 'No' to all that flouts the love of Christ, to every system, every programme and every person that treats anyone as though he or she were an irresponsible thing or a means of profit, to the defenders of injustice in the name of order, to those who sow the seeds of war or urge war as inevitable; 'Yes' to all that conforms to the love of Christ, to all who seek for justice, to the peace-makers, to all who hope, fight and suffer for the human cause, to all who — even without knowing it — look for new heavens and a new earth wherein dwelleth righteousness.

These tremendous words from that first World Council Assembly show so clearly that the ecumenical movement is not just concerned with unity in a narrow churchly sense, but with unity amongst all people. The imperative for Christian reconciliation lies at the heart of a Gospel for the whole world, a Gospel that a divided Church can only distort, corrupt and make ineffective.

The second Assembly of the World Council of Churches was held in Evanton (USA) in 1954. The report of this Assembly called the Churches to recognise and make far more of the unity latent behind all our divisions.

— *We all wait upon the one Father, through one Holy Spirit.*

- *We all read the Holy Scriptures and proclaim the Gospel from them.*
- *We all receive Christ's gift of baptism.*
- *We all hear his command to 'do this' and his word 'This is my body' ...*
  'this is my blood'.
- *We all receive a ministry of the Word and Sacraments.*
- *We are all called to be imitators of Christ.*

This means that though denominational Churches are still the dominant reality, 'the walls behind which they have taken shelter from one another are becoming transparent. The lines of division are shifting. There is a beginning of communication this way and that.'

The third Assembly of the World Council of Churches was held at New Delhi in India in 1961. The heart of its message was this:

> *We must together seek the fullness of Christian unity. We need for this purpose every member of the Christian family, of Eastern and Western tradition, ancient Churches and younger Churches, men and women, young and old, of every race and nation. Our brethren in Christ are given to us, not chosen by us. In some things our convictions do not yet permit us to act together, but we have made progress in giving content to the unity we seek.* Let us therefore find out the things which in each place we can do together now: and faithfully do them praying and working for that fuller unity which Christ wills for his Church.

This emphasis on unity in each place had been strongly made in the report of the section on Unity:

> *We believe that the unity which is both God's will and his gift to his Church is being made visible as all in each place who are baptised into Jesus Christ and confess him as Lord and Saviour are brought by the Holy Spirit into one fully committed fellowship.*

Small groups throughout the Churches in Scotland worked on these statements and tried to tease out the meaning of 'all in each place being brought into one fully committed fellowship'.

Here, for the first time, the local church in the local community is being seriously reckoned with. Unless and until there is an awakening amongst many more of the ordinary membership of the Churches, the ecumenical movement will be seen as a rare and specialist interest for theologians, moderators, bishops, but of little consequence in the ongoing life of the workaday parish.

Perhaps because of the treatment eventually meted out to the 'Bishops Report' in the 1950s, Church leaders in Scotland were more sensitive in this area than they might have been. It will be remembered that a most radical change had been proposed for the Presbyterian polity of the Church of Scotland: that a place be made for bishops within the Presbyterian structure and as a *quid pro quo* the Episcopal Church should take the lay eldership into its system. Despite a very clear and carefully worded report, despite the time given for study and discussion in the localities, despite the brilliant presentation and defence of the report in successive Assemblies by the Convener of the Joint Committee, Revd Dr Archie Craig, the response on the part of the Church of Scotland, ministry and membership, was decidedly negative.

The most important and most painful lesson for Scotland's ecumenical leaders in all this was the chasm it revealed between the leadership itself and the rank and file of ministers, elders and members. Edinburgh 1910 might have inaugurated a new age for the Protestant Church, but now, more than fifty years later, it was demonstrated beyond all question that the vision had hardly been glimpsed by any but a tiny minority of their fellow Christians throughout the Church.

It appeared to many in the 1950s and 60s that a great deal of our ecumenical talk and activities had simply served as a kind of inoculation against the 'glad infection of a new power for loving'. Again and again people said in discussions and debates on the Bishops Report that 'our rejection of these particular proposals does not mean the rejection of Christian unity or of our own or our Church's part in the ecumenical movement'. Such statements, however, without concrete alternative proposals, leave us with only the status quo of a denominationalism that had lost confidence in itself and had not yet found the faith to take the first practical steps towards something less destructive of the Gospel's calling to heal, to reconcile, to be God's peace-makers.

In September 1963 the Scottish Council of Churches convened a three day conference at St Andrews of representatives of all the mainstream Churches throughout the country. In the previous year a ten square-mile area around the old villages of Livingston and Livingston Station had been designated by the Government of the day as an area for development as a new town. One main finding of the St Andrews Conference was its unanimous recommendation to the Church authorities in Scotland not to assume that the old denominational pattern of Church life must be reproduced in the new town of Livingston, and instead to consider ways of encouraging right from the beginning the kind of transdenominational commitment to one another that will allow a more united Christian community to take shape in this particular locality.

This appeal was given strong backing by the All-Britain Churches Conference held in Nottingham in September of the following year. The plea was simply that as many as possible of the main denominations in Scotland should designate the new town of Livingston as an 'area of ecumenical experiment'.

As a result of an initiative taken by the parish minister of Livingston, David Torrance, the Presbytery of West Lothian succeeded in persuading the Home Board of the Church of Scotland to call together representatives of all the main-line Protestant denominations to consider the response they were prepared to make to the appeals from the St Andrews and Nottingham Conferences. The outcome of this initiative was that three historic denominations in Scotland – Congregational, Episcopal, Church of Scotland, to be followed later by a fourth, the Methodist – all agreed to treat Livingston as 'an area of ecumenical experiment', to share buildings and eventually to build an ecumenical centre in the town centre.

On 6th January 1966 the Livingston Ecumenical Experiment was officially launched by the induction/institution of the Church of Scotland minister and the Episcopal priest by Presbytery and Bishop functioning together for the first time in the history of our country.

So something unmistakably ecumenical, something that ordinary people could see and test for themselves, had been brought into being at the grassroots of urban life in Scotland. The following chapters in this book are one person's view of how that venture got off the ground and fared in the first twenty years or so, years that are notable not just for the decline of religious observance throughout the country, but also for the increase at a frightening pace of a materialistic view of life in which, as has so often been said, the verb 'to have' seems so much more important than the verb 'to be'. From the point of view of quick results and outward success this was quite the worst time to initiate anything in the life of the Church, except the most familiar and most immediately appealing, certainly not a time to launch out on a venture demanding deep-going changes in attitudes and outlook, in expectations and ways of working. It may not have been the best of times to move out from the safely traditional into the virtually unknown, but it could well have been God's time. The God of the Bible is so often the great disturber of people and their traditions, of Churches 'settled on the lees', of conscience and of the so-called keepers of the nation's conscience most of whom seem content that the new wine of the Gospel is still being kept in wine-skins so old and dry and hard that it is their very leakiness that prevents them bursting into pieces messily and noisily for everyone to see.

The Livingston Experiment has to do with people under the quickening influence of 'the Lord who is Spirit' doing a turnabout, a *metanoia*, from expending their energies on patching up the leaks to fashioning new skins for new wine.

CHAPTER 2

The God of Surprises

W HEN word got out in Airdrie, where we had been working for some eight years, that the Maitlands were to move to the new town of Livingston to take up work in the first ecumenical venture of its kind in Scotland, people would stop me in the street and say something like this: 'So you're leaving the West Parish and going to Livingston in West Lothian. Fine! But what kind of work are you going to be doing there? What is this "ecumenical experiment" mentioned in the papers? This could never mean that you're going to be worshipping with, working with ... *Catholics?*'

My response to this was unbelievably façile: 'Look! We can safely leave the Catholics to our children and our grandchildren. We have enough division on the Protestant side of the house to keep us fully occupied for our lifetime.'

This view of church life development in Scotland may have reassured our troubled parishioners in Airdrie. It certainly did not chime with the purposes of the Holy Spirit as, much to our surprise, we began to discover once we got properly started in the job in Livingston. One of the first assignments we found ourselves obliged to make was a visit to the Catholic Cardinal, Gordon Joseph Gray, in Edinburgh. The reason for that visit was quite simply to plead for two things:

First – that a Catholic priest be appointed to the new parish in Livingston as soon as possible and the usual practice of waiting until the new congregation was well on the way to economic viability be set aside.

Second – that serious consideration be given to the possibility of Catholic children being allowed to attend the one primary school for the parish with all the safeguards for instruction in the Catholic faith for the Catholic children duly noted and written into the agreement.

No one could have been more kindly or gracious than the Cardinal was that morning:

I have been giving much thought to this ecumenical development in Livingston. I am deeply interested and sympathetic, but the time is not ripe for us as Catholics to be formally associated with it so the question of shared schooling is just not discussable at this stage. As for the new priest, however, I have been thinking a great deal about this and I now have someone in mind who will work happily and amicably with the rest of you. I promise that he will be on the ground in Livingston before the end of this year.

The Cardinal was as good as his word. On 3rd December 1966 Father John Byrne moved into Livingston, into a house in Rannoch Walk just a few doors from our own.

It was the coming of John Byrne, with his friendliness, brightness and sparkling sense of humour, that made me begin to realise that whatever the official position of the Catholic Church with regard to Livingston's ecumenical project might be, with a priest of such warmth and humanity the Catholics here were going to be livingly concerned with the shaping of community life in the new town and inescapably therefore with its church life. Whatever else the Livingston way of trying to be the Church might signify, the Catholic priests and people were vitally caught up in it and to pretend otherwise would be quite unthinkable.

Three Stones

Up in the Bathgate hills, just north and west of Livingston, in fairly close proximity to each other, are three quite famous stones: the 'Sanctuary Stone', 'Preachers' Stane' and 'Witches' Hanging Stone'.

The Sanctuary Stone marks the boundary of the Torphichen Preceptory's 'field of influence'. For someone being pursued for alleged criminal activity, to reach this point meant safety from his persecutors and the right to a proper trial. It meant justice could be done and be seen to be done.

Around the Preachers' Stane the Covenanters of seventeenth century Scotland are said to have held their conventicles.

In between these two, stands a massive towering rock from which the witches were hanged. Even still, centuries later, the very sight of the place, shrouded as it is by the surrounding Caledonian firs, sends cold shivers of confusion and shame down the spine.

It is heartening to be reminded of the Mediaeval Church's concern to provide at least the beginnings of a way to serve the ends of justice, and allowing people and their society to emerge from being completely at the mercy of jungle law where it is each man for himself and the 'de'il tak' the hindmost'.

It is just as moving to be reminded of those who 'for the crown rights of the Redeemer' risked everything, even life itself, to win for themselves and their children the cornerstone of all the freedoms – freedom of worship.

The Witches' Hanging Stone, however, carries a very different message. It stands as a bleak reminder and warning of how easy it is for our concern for the Bible and its great imperatives on justice and freedom to be perverted to serve fanatical ends. Our debt as a people to the reformers of sixteenth and seventeenth century Scotland is quite unrepayable. But just as we see the complete distortion of Gospel faith in the hunting down and hanging of the witches by those who so stoutly proclaimed Reformation principles, so we have to see the sect-ridden mentality of so much church life in Scotland, on the Protestant side but also on the Catholic side, as a de-formation and denial of the word and the work of the Lord.

To turn our backs on fellow believers and set about building up separate, exclusive and often competing communities of the Lord's people may not be as harshly soul-curdling as the killing of the witches, but it is just as truly a denial of Gospel love and infinitely more damaging and far-reaching in its consequences. I doubt if we can ever assess properly the depth and extent of the hurt done to Scotland's community life by the dividedness and divisiveness of a Church as fragmented as ours has been for the last four hundred years.

We have always to be reminding ourselves and reminding one another that out-and-out adherence to so-called principle, to truth, or to that part of the truth as we perceive it, has to be tested and tempered by the Holy Spirit's leading and empowering, a leading and empowering that has always to do with healing and compassion, as well as with justice and freedom, with recognising and affirming the truth of the other person, the other religion, the other culture.

To those who take seriously the stress on righteousness at the heart of the Bible's teaching, the Witches' Hanging Stone, in all its grimness and terror, carries a powerful lesson still on the devilish consequences for us and our world when we leave out of the equation the controlling truth of the Gospel: that we are members one of another and if one member suffers – rejection, injustice, disparagement – we all suffer as persons, as families, as communities.

The Right Hand of Fellowship

Saint Paul tells a fascinating story of his own journey in the Way. In the first two chapters of his letter to the Galatians he recalls how he had been a rabid persecutor of the 'young Church' until 'it pleased God to reveal his Son in me so that I might preach him among the Gentiles'. Here is a turn up for the history books! A member of the most exclusive race on God's earth, a leading member of its strictest sect, the Pharisees, now making it his life's work to share with Romans, Greeks, Syrians … the accepting, new creating love of God in Christ, the Crucified and Risen One! This personal revelation is so wonderfully life-changing that once he has had time to come to terms with its meaning for him and his future, once he has had time to talk with and learn from the other Christians in Damascus, he gives himself, body and soul, to the preaching of this Gospel and the building up of its community for a period of some three years. Then, and not until then, he decides to go up to Jerusalem and there spends two weeks with Peter comparing notes, sharing experiences, strengthening each other's hands for the work.

Paul's way to faith in Christ had been very different from that of Peter and the rest of the disciples. The work to which he had been called – commending the Gospel to the Gentiles – had to be different from theirs, but Paul realised that whether in Jerusalem amongst the Jews or in Damascus amongst 'the lesser breeds without the Law', the work of Christ was one work and its unity had to be clearly and thankfully recognised and safeguarded. If he ever lost sight of this unity or treated it as secondary, then he would indeed have been running 'in vain' (Galatians 2: 2).

Paul is no freelance missionary. He insists that the work he is doing amongst these 'outsiders' – these Gentiles – is essentially the same as Peter, James and John are doing amongst the Jews of Jerusalem and elsewhere. To make this quite unmistakably clear to everyone concerned, Paul goes back to Jerusalem after 14 years preaching, teaching and strengthening the new believers amongst the Gentile peoples. His discussions there with the acknowledged leaders of the new movement convince both Paul and these leaders that, in their very different spheres of labour, they are all engaged in proclaiming the one message and sharing the one enterprise, for it is the one God in his Spirit who is at work in and through them all. In recognition of this essential oneness, the three Apostles give to Paul the right hand of fellowship (Galatians 2: 9) and he accepts this as sufficient warranty that, whatever the differences in their way of communicating the Gospel, they and he were comrades together in the service of the one Lord and his Kingdom and had to be seen as such.

This 'right hand of fellowship' was the *sine qua non* for Paul. Without it he would indeed have been running in vain and labouring in vain, would have been denied his true place in the 'fellowship of the Spirit', denied the love, the support, the prayers of these his fellow believers in God's 'new Messiah'.

So often we who stand in the tradition of the Reformation insist and go on insisting that there can never be anything like fruitful sharing or active and continuing co-operation between us and the people of the Catholic Church with its papacy, its authoritarian structures, its very different understanding of the Sacraments. These differences are undoubtedly there and are never to be glossed over, but are they anything like an adequate justification for our separate, often competitive, and sometimes quite hostile existence in the same community, in the same nation?

The Paul who is at such pains to make sure that he and his fellow Apostles in Jerusalem were, and were seen to be, yoke-fellows together in obedience to the one Lord, would have been dumbfounded and angry at the way we Protestants and Catholics have turned our backs on one another and go on, generation after generation, seemingly quite content to believe that there can be one God without one people of God, one Christ without there being one Body of Christ, and one Holy Spirit without one fellowship of that Spirit. Such deep-going division of Church life as we have perpetuated now for hundreds of years cannot but weaken, deform and make a nonsense of the Gospel we exist to proclaim.

What to do about all this? It is unthinkable for people who cherish the vision and achievements of the Reformation simply to return to Mother Church, the Roman Catholic Church. It is equally unthinkable for the Catholic Church so to abandon its understanding of God's Church in all the world and down the ages that Protestant and Orthodox Church people could begin to feel at home in it.

Is there a clue for us in St Paul's readiness to take the right hand of fellowship held out to him by the leaders of the Church in Jerusalem? The grounds for such a move, at local level and beyond, are stronger than we might imagine.

In recent years the Catholic Church has been clearly and repeatedly expressing strong positive appreciation of the contribution coming from the Protestant side to a much fuller understanding of the Christian faith.

> *Catholics must gladly acknowledge and esteem the truly Christian endowments for our common heritage which are to be found among our separated brethren. It is right and salutary to recognise the riches of Christ and virtuous works in the lives of others who are bearing witness to Christ, sometimes even to the shedding of their blood. For God is always wonderful in his works and worthy of all praise. Nor should we forget that anything wrought by the grace of the Holy Spirit in the hearts of our separated brethren can contribute to our own edification. Whatever is truly Christian is never contrary to what genuinely belongs to the faith; indeed it can always bring a more perfect realisation of the very mystery of Christ and the Church.*
>
> ~ From Vatican II, *Unitatis Kedintegratio* I. 4 ~

Several Catholic leaders and scholars have clearly acknowledged their own debt, and the debt of other thinking Christians, to Protestant exegetical work on different Bible passages, as well as to work done within Protestant circles on Christian ethics, particularly social ethics.

This recognition of the Spirit's authentic witness outwith the bounds of the Catholic Church itself is of the very greatest consequence not only for future developments within that Church, but for the nurture of new attitudes and hopes amongst all who belong to that part of the Church that the reformers themselves saw not as the Church reformed in a completed and final sense, but always as the Church being reformed. Could not this continuing reformation now and in the coming century consist primarily of finding and deepening new relationships of trust and thankfulness and healing love?

If Catholic attitudes to their 'separated brethren' have changed radically in the past fifty years, is there not now a pressing obligation on us as the 'Children of the Reformation' to acknowledge humbly and penitently the unmistakable signs of the Holy Spirit's work and leading within the Catholic Church?

The saints and martyrs of that Church are not all of long ago but of today. Take but one example …

Archbishop Romero of El Salvador was assassinated at his prayers in church on 25th March 1980. Words of his uttered shortly before his death have the ring of Gospel assurance, of Gospel defiance of ruthless, irresponsible power: 'May my blood be a seed of freedom and the sign that hope will soon be a reality.' A Church that gives a testimony as clear and courageous as this must itself be an active participant in the Holy Spirit's working in and for the life of the world.

If we as Catholics and Protestants are to find the Spirit-given willingness to offer to and receive from each other the right hand of fellowship, we must be as prepared as Paul and Barnabas were to make real personal contact with one another, to make time to listen to one another, to be quiet together before the Lord and start to learn from him, the meek and lowly-hearted Christ of God, what he wants us to be doing together with him and for his Kingdom in our own communities, in our own towns and districts.

Together for the Kingdom

Whatever else the Gospel teaches, it teaches this – that we can only count properly for the Lord and his work as we go at it together.

At the beginning of his ministry Jesus uses the teaching and experience of the prophets to set forth his own charter to the people in the synagogue at Nazareth, the very village where he had been brought up and laboured for years as a carpenter: The love of God is not just for Israel but goes spilling out to people in their need, whatever their race, whatever their religion (Luke 4: 16-30).

In the Sermon on the Mount – in Matthew 5: 23,24 (NIV) – Jesus says:

> *If you are offering your gift at the altar and there remember that your brother has something against you, leave the gift there in front of the altar. First go and be reconciled to your brother; then come and offer your gift.*

There is something bogus about worship that leaves out of the reckoning the people who, for whatever reason, are no longer our people. 'First go and be reconciled with your estranged brother. Then and only then will our Father God be able to accept and fully bless our worship.' Without the unity our Lord wants and wills for his people the Churches cannot but go on cheating one another and cheating the world of its best chance ever of coming to faith.

All this – and much more – is there 'in the Book' and is read or heard again and again wherever God's word is proclaimed. But little or nothing ever seems to happen in consequence of being brought under that word. We just go on following the age-old routine that keeps us apart and makes us such a blockage to the river of God's justice and the power of God's healing.

My own experience is this – we can go on forever deploring our wretched divisions, but we are never likely to make one significant step towards actual reconciliation until we personally begin to meet one another across the divide. Then we can start discovering for ourselves that these strangers who have been so highly suspect are really our brothers/sisters who need us as much as we need them.

The present-day ghetto lifestyle of the different Churches is, in my view, ecumenical enemy number one. The far-reaching influence of Livingston's first parish priest, Father John Byrne, has already been mentioned. His own special charisma was the genuineness of his love for people and his ability to make them feel accepted and valued. His successors at St Andrew's, Craigshill – Charlie Barclay and John Creanor – have strongly maintained the openness towards the surrounding community that made Father Byrne so greatly beloved and such a power for peace and reconciliation. In this context it is almost impossible for friendships between Catholics and Protestants, priests and ministers, not to develop and these friendships are, as I believe, the very stuff of the living social tissue that renewal of Christian unity could begin to give to both church and community life in Scotland.

The coming of Father John Robinson to St Peter's Church in Carmondean in 1992 marked the opening of a new chapter in Livingston's understanding and experience of ecumenical relationships. Here was a parish priest who, more than any other I have ever known, had a passionate commitment to the recovery of the Church's lost unity. He had a Church of Scotland minister to 'preach him in' at the official inaugural service of his ministry at St Peter's. He was the moving spirit behind the revival of the old Fraternal now called the Ministers' Fellowship, and had us going three times a year for a day's conference and retreat in Cross House, Linlithgow. It was out of one of these that the first arrangement was made for priests, ministers and people to meet for prayer at 12 noon on the Thursdays of Lent, and for that day to forgo a midday meal, giving the money thus saved to Christian Aid. He became secretary to the Livingston Council of Churches and managed this work so well that, for the first time ever, a group of 25 Catholics and Protestants in Livingston spent a week together on Iona looking at the possibilities of achieving full inter-communion amongst all the mainline Churches by the beginning of the new millennium.

My wife and I used to go from time to time to the St Peter's 11.30 Mass on a Sunday morning. Our presence in the congregation, our actively taking part in all the worship but prevented from sharing the Lord's bread and cup, troubled him deeply. So that we would not feel we had been sent empty away, quite often Father John would provide 'blessed bread' which he would give to each of us with his priestly blessing. 'In this way,' he used to say, 'we are seeing to it that no one has to go hungry from the feast of our Lord's appointing.'

In the summer of 1994 Father John was felled by illness and obliged to take a sabbatical year completely away from parish work. Our hope and constant prayer is that this dear man of God will be sent back to us in Livingston. But whether here or elsewhere, his life and word and witness will be clear testimony to the reality of the Spirit's working to make his people one.

Two Learning Experiences

Readers will remember how, at the very beginning of the Livingston Ecumenical Experiment, a strong plea was made to Cardinal Gray in Edinburgh that Catholic children in the new parish be allowed to share schooling with their Protestant brothers and sisters in a non-denominational building. The plea was politely but firmly dismissed, and the subject, while never completely lost sight of, had to be shelved as too sensitive for open discussion. For some of us this concern remained as an issue that still rankled and one that was not likely to disappear in the forseeable future.

In 1993 Father John Robinson arranged for me to be present at the Catholic Primary School for Carmondean and Knightsridge during the celebration Mass for the school's patron saint, John Ogilvie.

What, for me, was so impressive about this celebration was not the presence of so many clergy, from the Archbishop down, but the active participation of the children in the entire service and most especially the way in which all the children over seven years of age went forward to share the bread and wine of the Eucharist. You only had to see the look on the children's faces as they returned to their places in class to know immediately that for every one of them this indeed was for real. So true was this that everyone present, adults and children, felt themselves caught up in a liberating work of the Spirit that allowed us not only to know the Lord's nearness but to share a tasting of the love that 'is very patient, very kind and never fails', the very love that makes us kith and kin to one another whatever denominational labels we may carry around. I came away from that celebration humbled and deeply thankful, but also vexed and troubled in mind: Why have we Protestants failed to preserve for our children anything comparable in spiritual worth?

How can we begin to regain the ground that has been so completely lost?

How can we find the confidence that will allow us make a start on this with the openness, penitence and urgency the situation demands?

My long and deeply-held conviction on the need for integrated schooling between Catholics and Protestants remains, but the simplistic and unexamined nature of that conviction now calls, for me at least, to make 'agonising reappraisal' right across the board of educational provision.

To make a start on this requires, as I see it, a quiet, patient and prayerful coming together on the part of ordinary people from both sides in Scotland's household of faith, with priests and ministers contributing as they can. Some Northern Ireland schools – like Laggan College – have much to teach us in this regard.

One of the Least of These

The other experience I want to mention is this:

Our youngest grandson was born with Down's Syndrome. When the time came for him to start primary school, his parents were faced with deciding which of the local schools would best meet his educational needs: the School for Special Needs, the Non-Denominational Primary or the Catholic Primary. After visiting the three schools and talking with different teachers, they slowly and somewhat reluctantly came to the conclusion that for their Andrew the Catholic school seemed to have the edge on the others. They felt that the atmosphere there had a relaxed lightness about it and a complete absence of hard driving competitiveness. There they felt their child stood a good chance of being accepted as a person in his own right, with something to give as well as a great deal to receive. And how right they were! Andrew's confidence increased steadily, his ability to communicate verbally with those around him improved by the day, while his happiness at being 'one of the boys' in his class shone through his every look and gesture. What was especially encouraging – and so unexpected – was the way the teachers, from the Head down, kept insisting that 'Andrew has done far more for us as a school than we could ever do for him'.

There is not a shadow of doubt in my own mind that this quality of loving community flows from and is nurtured by Gospel belief and practice. That this is happening, even in small pockets of Scottish education, must be seen as a challenge to our educationalists and politicians, but most of all to the parents and concerned men and women in our local communities. The potential for the rescue of children so incredibly exposed to abuse of all kinds, flagrant and genteel, is undoubtedly available to those who are prepared to plead and strive and pray for such radical reform of our common life as will allow us to begin to discover all over again what it really means to 'love our neighbour as ourselves'.

End Piece – Words attributed to Martin Luther

If I profess with the loudest voice and clearest exposition every portion of the truth of God except precisely that little point where the world and the devil are at the moment attacking, I am not confessing Christ, however boldly I may be professing Christ. Where the battle rages there the loyalty of the soldier is proved, and to be steady on all the battlefield besides, is mere flight and disgrace if he flinches at that one point.

Would anyone in these times, when we are standing at the end of the most murderous century in the history of humankind, deny that 'that little point where the world and the devil are at the moment attacking' most fiercely and destructively is the very point where division – ethnic, religious, social, economic – is most cleverly in evidence. To let the Gospel of the God of peace be heard as good news of deliverance in these very areas where the battle has been going against us all to the going down of the sun, the people of Christ – especially the Catholic and Protestant people of Christ – must in a clear and simpler way turn to God and to one another in repentance and childlike expectancy of new light 'from the Lord who is Spirit'.

The Spirit lives to set us free,
walk, walk in the light.
He binds us all in unity,
walk, walk in the light.

Walk in the light,
walk in the light,
walk in the light,
walk in the light of the Lord.

CHAPTER 3

Lighting a Candle

THE first ever conference on Livingston and its ecumenical venture was held in Scottish Churches House, Dunblane in the summer of 1967 when the project was little more than a year old. For me, the most significant utterance made at the conference came not from the ministers, the theologians, nor the 'ecumaniacs', but from Malcolm Drummond, Landscape and Forestry Officer with the Livingston Development Corporation – and the first Session Clerk to the new church in Livingston made up of people from the Scottish Congregational Union, the Scottish Episcopal Church, the Methodist Church and the Church of Scotland (Presbyterian). In the midst of a lively discussion on the work of what was then called the 'Livingston Ecumenical Experiment', Malcolm said: 'For us in Livingston, the church is the community and the community is the church.'

The clerics, and perhaps some others, were shocked and tut-tutted at such a theological nonsense, but the contingent from Craigshill, the first area of the new town to be developed and the place where 'it was all happening', accepted Malcolm's description as accurate and of vital importance for understanding the nature of the work on the ground and of the radical difference the ecumenical dimension makes to our commitment as the people of the Church.

The word 'ecumenical' is derived directly from the Greek *oikumene,* meaning the 'whole inhabited world'. Those who begin to discern the ecumenical nature of our calling as Christians have to be helping one another to recognise and to break free from the captivity of the Churches to their own deadly institutionalism with all its inward-lookingness and self-concern.

Jesus spoke constantly about the Kingdom of God. He taught his followers to look for the signs of its living presence, like the moving, disturbing influence of yeast in a great lump of dough.

More than that, he taught that religious people themselves, however sincere and pious, could be the greatest obstacle to a fuller coming of that Kingdom. So he called everyone to repent – synagogue-attenders, temple worshippers, as well as 'publicans and sinners'. He called them to turn right around, to turn away from exclusive prayings and preachings and endless efforts to manipulate the Lord of Heaven and earth. 'Come with me,' he said, 'learn of me. I will give you new eyes to look on the world about you and see it as God's world and all its people as his people.'

We used to say that in the little Craigshill parish of Livingston, West Lothian we had just the beginnings of a real parish church that had hardly been seen in Scotland since the days of the Reformation. This tiny, tiny bit of God's global village is, in a very real sense, entrusted to the people of the Kingdom as they come together under the word of the Gospel, as they share together the Lord's bread and cup, as they go out to be, through their togetherness in the fellowship of the Spirit – *light* and *leaven* and *salt*. *Light* that has love in it; *leaven* that is the living grace of God working through our struggles, our looks, our words and half-words; *salt* that has marvellous God-given powers to prevent corruption and give fresh savour to our daily living.

The Promised Land

For close on thirty years, my wife Elizabeth and I have been sharing new town life in Livingston. Many strong negative criticisms have been made of the new town concept and some have real validity. We must never forget, however, or allow our country and its political leaders to forget, how the new town idea came to birth in twentieth century Britain.

During the early months of the Second World War, when everyone expected the bombing of our cities to happen right away, the children of these cities were 'evacuated' in their thousands to the safety of rural areas where people, with utmost goodwill, received them into their homes and schools and churches. The immediate and utterly unexpected effect was one of shock and horror at the state of so many of these children – dirty, neglected, poverty-stricken in body, mind and soul. The outcry over this was so passionate and widespread that the authorities were compelled to take notice and to make solemn declaration that, once the war was over, there would be a new deal for the children of our inner cities and their parents. This new deal would take the form of purpose-built new towns, all of them to express in some clear way the vision of the 'Garden City' that would wipe out forever the degradation of slumdom and all that went with it – for the slum-dweller and for those who were prepared to allow it, ignore it, excuse it.

People who have lived in any one of Scotland's new towns have ample reason to be endlessly thankful for the consequences of the children's 'exodus' from the cities at the outbreak of the Second World War, for in many big and positive ways new town living, despite many lacks and limitations, has been a taste for multitudes of 'the promised land' itself. Here are trees and greenness and gardens and space. Our new towns are one unmistakable expression of a nation's repentance for sinning against God and the people made in his likeness, sinning that began with the Industrial Revolution and went on for more than a century.

Social Conscience

I have often found myself wondering what kind of dumbfounding shock, comparable to that brought about by the flood of juvenile deprivation suddenly sweeping down on the nice, respectable, comfortable people of Scotland's country districts, would need to happen today to stab our consciences awake to the plight of our society and its fateful consequences for us all and especially for our children?

Some of us were naïve enough to wonder if the murder of James Bulger by children not yet in their teens, might horrify us enough to take a fresh, hard, searching look at ourselves in our culture of single-parent poverty, of grudging concern for the weakest among us, of inadequate education, sexual harassment, rape, and child abuse. This did not happen. There has been far stronger correspondence in the press over the siting of the new Scottish Gallery of National Art, or even over credal correctness in the Church of Scotland's profession of faith, than resulted from the revelation of the death-working powers of evil to which our children are so increasingly exposed. Of course art galleries and their proper siting are important, and so is the Churches' creed, but these fade into insignificance, if not complete irrelevance, in the face of the increasing bedevilment that seems to be taking over great areas of our common life.

Perhaps the kind of change required cannot or will not come about through some nationwide experience of shock and dismay, but quite slowly and unspectacularly through two or three or five people here, there, all over the place, beginning to share some fresh insights from their own sharing of the Lord's hunger and thirst to see justice done, or beginning to be done, for all his children in all his world.

Ordinary people – the more ordinary the better – coming together in their own locality quite simply and honestly to look for ways of seeking a fuller coming of God's Kingdom in their own community, their nation, their world – especially and most urgently – the Third World – all such seeking folk will quickly be led to see where and how they must work, who they must work with, learn from, give support to, through their active presence and their constant prayers. A famous continental Church leader used to say that the prime missionary task for the Church today is not to fish for people with a line, nor with a net, but to change, to cleanse, the waters of the fishing grounds. If the fish are slowly being poisoned through polluted seas, all fishing is doomed. If the social atmosphere of our Scottish communities is so polluted as to be life-threatening to so much that really matters for the health of our common life, every community must pay serious attention.

Every community must find ways of encouraging groups of their own people to reach out to one another across racial, social, religious divides and see how they can begin to explore together the challenging possibilities in a more neighbourly way of living.

Livingston's Forum

Livingston with its ecumenical parish is, as I believe, of immense importance for everyone searching for a means of renewal of community life as well as church life throughout our country.

Being a new church in a new town helped many of us make the all-important discovery that, like it or lump it, the needs, the problems, the aspirations of the people all around have to be given priority over every thing else. Endlessly we quoted to ourselves and anyone else who would listen, the words of P. T. Forsyth, theological scholar and prophet of the Congregational Church in England: 'Jesus came not to save souls, not to found churches, but so to save souls, so to found churches, that there might be righteous communities and righteous nations.'

We had been given a flying start in Livingston, for our parent bodies – the Episcopal, Congregational, Methodist Churches and the Church of Scotland – had all agreed that, for the work in this new town, they would share buildings in the different areas and eventually erect an Ecumenical Centre in the town centre.

This was a minimal commitment to Christian unity, but it was sufficient to allow us to have a team ministry and to share not just buildings but the work and the planning of the work, mid-week prayers and the Sunday services.

Two initiatives were taken in the first months. First, a weekly broadsheet called *News Flash* was circulated to every home so that we could all know what was happening and when and where. Second, a Sunday morning Forum was set up for everyone who wanted to get to know their neighbours, for everyone who had a problem, a criticism, a suggestion to make about our life as a new town. This Forum quickly became the living heart of the new community. It met for an hour in the one public building available – Riverside Primary School. On a Sunday morning there were church services, Catholic and Episcopal, at 9.30; and Catholic and Church of Scotland services at 11.30; and in between the Forum met. The one feature of this gathering, emphasised right at the beginning and constantly thereafter, was that it was there for everyone – Protestant and Catholic, church and unchurched, the community-minded and those who quite simply had some kind of realisation that in this new town the well-being of one was somehow bound up with the well-being of all. It was this strengthening sense of belonging that appealed so strongly and helped to give people the gut-feeling that they mattered and that their questions, difficulties and ideas mattered as well. 'We may make a kirk or a mill of it, but we're all in it together.'

Many of the problems brought to Forum could be dealt with immediately and in quite practical ways. How eagerly people responded to the needs expressed and how readily they would give not just advice but the use of tools for the house – for example, a power drill, or implements for tackling the mud-patch waiting to be made into a garden.

Often the issues raised required action from one of the two authorities responsible for this part of the new town, Livingston Development Corporation and the Midlothian County Council. Always a small *ad hoc* group was appointed from among ourselves to make the necessary approaches and to report to the next meeting. Three big concerns dominated Forum's working over the next three years. At this distance they seem small beer indeed, but for us at the time in a new town community struggling to find its own identity, they were vitally important. These were: leaking flats, high school education, and household rubbish disposal.

Leaking Flats

During the Summer 1965 the Forum received constant complaints from residents in the 'system built' flats. Whenever there was a moderate rainfall, livingroom, bedrooms, kitchen would have water running down the walls. The housing officers in the Development Corporation kept telling us that the work was in hand and the matter was being dealt with. But the water kept coming in and, during a rainstorm, flooded down the walls. After weeks of waiting in vain for some kind of effective remedial action, Forum decided that the matter was serious enough for us to appeal to our Member of Parliament, Alex Eadie. Alex soon proved himself a wise and supportive friend and champion. On his advice, Forum arranged for the Board members and officials of the Development Corporation to attend its meeting on a Sunday morning in the main hall of Riverside Primary School. The Chairman and Board members were angry and upset, partly, we thought, because instead of finding a handful of 'damp sufferers', they found the great school hall packed to capacity and overflowing. Despite the negative and sometimes quite combative nature of that encounter, the Board at the end of it held an emergency meeting and made these significant decisions:

- Every tenant affected by damp would be offered alternative accommodation forthwith.
- The Board would be responsible for removal expenses.
- The Board would pay compensation for all furnishings spoilt by damp.

This positive response heartened us all. It soon became clear that the entire episode of the leaking flats, and Forum's part in dealing with it, did more than anything else to deepen the feeling of solidarity amongst the residents.

High School Education

The other big public concern brought to Forum had to do with plans for the opening of the new High School. The Midlothian Education Committee had decided that, for the first few years, Craigshill High would be treated as an annexe of West Calder High, and for that period the Head Teacher of the new school would be the Head at West Calder High and the principal teachers of the main departments there would be responsible for the same departments in Craigshill.

Forum immediately protested against this decision and elected a strong *ad hoc* group to approach the Education Committee and convey to it the feelings of the parents and others in Craigshill. The Committee responded very positively and appointed a sub-committee, including the Director of Education, to meet with Forum's representatives in Craigshill. This sub-committee spent an entire evening putting their case and listening to ours. The upshot was the over-turn of the original decision and the agreement of the full Committee to appoint a Head Teacher without delay and to have four principal teachers in place for the actual opening of the school.

This achievement on the part of Forum did a great deal to boost the morale of the town and, more importantly, helped us all to recognise even then the reality of 'people power'.

Household Rubbish Disposal

Let no one imagine for a moment that Forum was a success story from beginning to end. We had our dismal failures and this was one. We pled as hard and as often as we could with West Lothian's cleansing department to arrange an extra uplift from the rubbish bin store-room on the ground floor of every block of flats. A weekly collection meant that, in summertime especially, the entry and stairs could be overwhelmingly offensive. Despite our pleas having the strong backing of our medical doctor and district nurse, the cleansing department remained adamant in their refusal. They would provide an extra bin bag, but no extra uplift. After months of meetings and pleadings we gave up, telling ourselves that we would return to this business at a later date – but we never did.

If you were to speak with anyone who was around in Craigshill in these first three years (1966-69), s(he) would tell you that what was so remarkable about life in this brand new community was the strong sense we all had of being members together in a shared venture for the common good. People felt that they were accepted and appreciated and were being counted on 'to be there with and for one another'. How aware and how responsive 'ordinary' people are to this kind of atmosphere. Undoubtedly the main contributor to all this was Sunday morning's Forum, where the conventional barriers – social, religious, ethnic, political – had no place. Here the Catholic priest and the Protestant ministers, the agnostic social worker and the young radical activist, were all equally at home.

Brian Keenan, in his book *An Evil Cradling*, says this of life in Belfast as he knew it: 'A kind of malevolence festered and spread uncontrollably and unseen.' With us in these first years of new town living, something the very opposite of this deeply affected us all. A dynamic friendliness and good-neighbourliness seemed to be present everywhere and everyone was contributing to its felt reality.

What brought all this about; and why, after some three years, did it grow thin and then all but disappear?

The first reason for this spirit of fellowship being so strong was the existence of the new town itself and the realisation that we all had responsibility for creating and maintaining traditions of caring and active citizenship. This depended on us and on no one else.

The second reason for this sense of community was that four historic Church denominations in Scotland had people in Livingston who were ready to do more than just share buildings. They were involved together with others in trying to give shape and purpose to the life of the surrounding community. The Churches' concern for the well-being of all – Catholics and Protestants, the unchurched as much as the church-goer – was given an even clearer expression by the Team Ministry, consisting at that stage of three full-time ministers – Brian Hardy of the Scottish Episcopal Church, Hamish Smith of the Congregational Church in Scotland, myself as the Church of Scotland minister, and Max Cruikshank, the Church of Scotland Youth Worker.

The third reason for this community feeling lay with the one building – the Riverside Primary School. Here everything of a communal nature had to happen, and here on Sundays people didn't just gather for church services. Through Forum they met one another, talked with one another and gradually built up relationships of a kind that were sometimes described as 'each for all and all for each'. Because we were all able to meet, and did meet every Sunday morning at Forum, our separating up for different Church Services before and after the Forum gathering came to seem almost irrelevant. The living heart of our community life was not in any worship service, but in our grassroots parliament and the comradeship it generated.

Fragmentation

Why did this feeling of community, of our belonging to one another, begin to fade and die after some three years? ('Die' is undoubtedly too strong a word. 'Hibernate' might be nearer the truth, with its suggestion of waiting through the winter of our discontent for the return of Spring.)

The main reason for this fade-out was, as I believe, the move on the part of the two congregations to their own building: the ecumenical people to St Columba's in 1969 and the Catholics shortly afterwards to St Andrew's. However well-intentioned priests/ ministers and their congregations may be about the claims of the civil community and its affairs, the very fact of their operating from separate centres deprives people around of the signs and stirrings of that wholeness that is the very stuff of real community.

This rather daunting experience helped some of us on the ecumenical side of things to realise that our denominational divisions not only deprived the Church of something quite essential to its calling as the people of God, but, even more importantly, it deprived the local community of powers and influence that could be making for livelier, more inclusive community living. Perhaps the greatest sin of the Church in Scotland in the past five hundred years is seen not in what it has done to itself as 'the fellowship of the Holy Spirit', but in what it has done to the life of our local communities by denying them the opportunity of discerning in their midst the human reality of the Gospel of God's invading Kingdom the very essence of which is accepting, reconciling, new-creating love.

As I see it, the true worth of Forum's contribution to the life of the new town in these first years of its existence was that it gave many of us a fresh and stimulating taste of what 'life together' could mean for every person and every family and for the entire locality. A new feeling of being freed-up by, with and for one another allowed us to participate personally and directly in the exhilarating, if sometimes quite daunting, work of seeking for this town of ours an undergirding sense of purpose and corporate identity.

CHAPTER 4

Spill-over from the First Three Years

THE move away from the one public building by the Churches put paid to Forum and the warm liveliness of its community concern. The spirit of good neighbourliness, however, bred and nurtured by these Sunday morning meetings, made the people who shared that experience much more sensitive and responsive to the families in their street, and especially to newcomers as they tried to settle in amongst us. In a very real sense these early residents, whether they stayed on in Craigshill or moved to new areas like Howden, Ladywell, or Dedridge, were, in a quite unselfconscious way, a leaven of friendliness and positive goodwill.

These years in Riverside Primary School taught many of us that the basic ingredient for better ecumenical understanding and growth is not endless statement and restatement of theological beliefs and doctrines, important as that must always be, but the experience of genuine friendships across denominational divides at local parish level. Where that is happening, the spirit of healing, the spirit of peace can and does operate often in ways that are deeply and lastingly real. Again and again we have found, particularly in the last few years, that the most Spirit-filled acts of worship we ever take part in are those where Protestants and Catholics are engaged together in waiting on the Lord and seeking his way for themselves, their churches, their community. What is perhaps most remarkable is the evident joy that people can come to find in ways of praying and worshipping that are very different from those followed in their own tradition.

All this amounts to is quite simply that the larger place we can give to the leading of God's Spirit as it is brought to us in the Bible and the happenings of our own time, the less room there can ever be for denominational exclusiveness. Receptive openness to others is indeed the name of the game in the calling of God's people today.

Lanthorn

One far-reaching consequence of the Forum years made itself known when the third of the churches' buildings in Livingston came to be erected.

When the ecumenical project was launched, the parent bodies of the Churches involved had agreed that the Church of Scotland would be responsible for putting up the first building (St Columba's in Craigshill); the Scottish Episcopal Church for the second (St Paul's in Ladywell/Howden); and the Scottish Congregational Union for the third, in the Dedridge area. It should be noted that, right from the beginning, the fourth member of the co-operating churches – the Methodist Church in Scotland – decided that there would be no question of Methodists putting up a building of any kind in Livingston. In the event, however, the Methodist Church contributed most generously to two of Livingston's church buildings – Mosswood in Knightsridge and the recently opened worship centre in Carmondean.

The first two buildings were of a more or less traditional pattern and have served well the ecumenical congregations in their respective areas. Hamish Smith was the Congregationalist member of the Team Ministry. He had read more clearly than any of us the sign for our times in these three years of sharing one building, where that sharing involved the constant meeting and mixing of people from very different social and religious backgrounds, as well as people of no religious persuasion whatsoever. So Hamish was led to share with us all his vision of a building in Dedridge that would be as much for the community as for the churches. Before he was able to begin to work out the practical details of his vision, Hamish was called to be full-time chaplain to Edinburgh University and his place in the Team Ministry was taken by another Congregationalist minister, Ross McLaren of East Kilbride, the first of Scotland's new towns.

Ross was delegated the humanly impossible task of giving another person's dream acceptable embodiment in bricks and mortar. He took up the challenge with single-minded conviction and succeeded not only in working with and through the different local authorities (District Council, Regional Council and Livingston

Development Corporation), but also, much to the surprise of myself and many others, in persuading the Catholic Church to be part of the new complex and to share a central worship space with the ecumenical congregation. The end result thrilled us all – a building housing the Dedridge Public Library, offering every kind of facility for the people of the community and the people of the churches.

The name chosen for the new centre was 'Lanthorn' – *ie* bearer of a fragile, trembling light giving fresh glimpses of a way in which we can find one another and affirm one another as members together of the one neighbourhood.

It should be noted that the two new churches opened since the advent of Lanthorn – that of Mosswood in Knightsridge and the building for the ecumenical congregation in Carmondean – both express, in quite different ways, the Lanthorn concept of church and community togetherness. The true benefits of this way of integrating church and parish concern will only begin to come into its own and be properly appreciated for the potential in its witness to the essential wholeness of our common life, when the churches, Protestant and Catholic, in any one area, give themselves to one another and to the surrounding community in more adventurous, more prayerful caring for every soul, every family within the bounds. How much help we need from one another, from God's word in the Bible, from God's Spirit in prayer and sacrament, to make us more eager, more expectant servants not of a religious denomination, but of him who is the bringer of God's life-renewing Kingdom to our own locality, to our nation, to our world!

A Fuller Communion

The third great consequence of the Forum years has to do with the heart of Church belief and practice. The people of the four co-operating denominations – Episcopal, Church of Scotland, Congregational, Methodist – had come to an early agreement that their worship needs on a Sunday morning would be met by:

– A celebration of the Eucharist according to the Episcopal order at 9.30 am every Sunday;

- A communion service on the first Sunday of each month at 11.30 am.
- A 'preaching service' on all the other Sundays.

All these services were to be held in the main hall of Riverside Primary School.

This arrangement seemed to be working well enough with, on most Sundays, a handful of us from the so-called non-liturgical churches attending at 9.30, but never able to share Communion. The change in all this was brought about not by pleas or protests on the part of the clergy, but by the 'lay people' themselves. A group of the regular worshippers at the 9.30 Eucharist asked for an interview with the then bishop, Ken Carey. In the course of that interview, they said something like this:

> *In Livingston the church people work together in everything affecting the life of the parish, irrespective of denomination. We visit in the streets, we teach the children, we plan the work, and we pray for the work at the mid-week prayer service. At only one point are we separate and kept apart, and that is at the Lord's table. Please, Bishop, can you see a way of putting an end to this glaring anomaly?*

As a result of this approach, the bishop, in a matter of weeks, gave what he called his 'encouragement' to the Episcopal priest and people in Livingston to invite to full participation in their celebration of Holy Communion the members of the other three denominations in the Ecumenical Parish. He also made it clear that it would be in order for the ministers of these denominations to preside at celebrations of the eucharist following the Episcopal order.

Diversity's Benefits

This breakthrough did more than anything else not only to transform and vitalise our Church relations, but to open up quite practical ways of appreciating the riches in the different traditional practices.

For example – in the Episcopal Church, members receive communion not sitting in their pews, but kneeling or standing out front. They receive directly from the officiating priest with some such word as 'The body of Christ', 'The blood of Christ'. This is not to imply that the episcopal way of celebrating is somehow better. It is simply different and for many, many people is deeply meaningful.

One particular practice had immediate appeal. At the point of making Communion, parents and their children are invited to come forward together. The parents and children who have been confirmed are given the Sacrament with the word 'The body of Christ', 'The blood of Christ'. The younger children, in a parent's arms or kneeling beside, have the minister's hand laid on their head with the word 'The blessing of Christ'.

Could anything be more strengthening for the bonds of family life than such a practice week-in–week-out?

This opening up of the Lord's table took place in October 1968 when we were still worshipping in the school building. We found that both there, and later in the St Columba's building, people from the non-Episcopal side often out-numbered the Episcopalians themselves. What a spiritually profitable exercise it is to put oneself in the shoes of those standing in a quite different tradition from your own. It demands patience and effort and a readiness to learn and relearn, but how richly rewarding it can prove.

It was providential that for these crucial opening years, the Episcopal member of the Team Ministry was Brian Hardy, a man of remarkable musical gifts and so 'far ben' spiritually that people felt an authentic ring in everything he said. They quickly felt at home with him, whether he was presiding at the Episcopal Eucharist or preaching the Word at a Church of Scotland service.

People from other Countries and Cultures

From the very beginning, ours was a 'mixed' population. People from Glasgow and Edinburgh found that, beyond the teasing and pretend-boasting, there was a real enjoyment of each other's company. Families from south of the border were as enthusiastic as any in the work to make this not just another new town, but a place where people were discovering what it takes to make glad acceptance of one another and be eager to appreciate the contributions coming out of different backgrounds and experience. We shall be saying more about the Patel family later, but let us note here how deeply thankful they were to have their home in Livingston after several months of trying to get by as newcomers in a vast city conglomerate like London.

An unforgettable lesson in this kind of openness now required between governors and governed, neighbour and neighbour, nation and nation, was given to us at the first Service of Remembrance held in Riverside School on Remembrance Sunday 1966. We had no parade, no flags or pipes or drums. Just the people of the place gathered for Forum, and later for worship. But we kept our two minutes silence and we talked a little about peace, peace-making and peace-keeping. Our invited speaker for the occasion was Pepi Fried, who with his wife and two boys had recently moved into the town and made their home in a Rannoch Walk flat, a few hundred yards from our own house in the same street.

Pepi told us about his own country, Czechoslovakia, and how he had had to spend several of his childhood years in a Hitler detention camp. He told us about training for his life's work as an architect, how he had met and married a Scots artist, Ann Shortreed, and how the birth of his two sons, Michael and Peter, had brought a new depth of meaning and happiness into their own lives. He also made much of his awareness of a religious dimension to Scottish life and culture not nearly so evident in his own country, a dimension that in some ways was repressive and inhibiting in its effects.

His message for peace was very simple: 'People,' he insisted, 'are greater than the systems in which they have to live and work and this means there is hope for Czechoslovakia, for Scotland, for the world.'

That could have had a platitudinous ring if it had been uttered by a Scots preacher like myself. But coming as it did from one who had suffered, whose family had suffered, and whose Jewish people had been subjected to unspeakable horrors by the ruthless working of an evil system of government, such a word conveyed to us all on that Remembrance Sunday a belief in the worth, the infinite worth, of ordinary men and women and their powers to win through to an ultimate destiny that has peace at its heart. That bedrock faith was still there in Pepi Fried, despite his frequent insistences on being still completely without religion of any kind. The faith of his forbears nurtured for generations by the teachings and sufferings of Israel's prophets and lawgivers was still the profoundest influence on his life and outlook.

Dietrich Bonhoeffer, in *Letters and Papers from Prison* (SCM, 1950), wrote this shortly before his death at the hands of Hitler's hangmen:

I believe
that God both can and will bring good out of evil.
For that purpose God needs men and women who will make the best
use of everything.
I believe
that God is willing to provide us in any emergency with all the powers
of resilience that will be necessary for us.
But he will not give in advance
lest we should rely upon ourselves and not on him alone.
It is such a faith that will overcome all anxiety and fear of the future.
I believe
that God is not a timeless fate
but that he is attending and responding
to sincere prayer as well as to responsible action.

A First Community Council

Despite the serious loss for church and community brought about by the move into separate buildings, the feeling of friendliness and good neighbourliness generated by Forum continued to make themselves felt. One outcome of this, the worth of which has never been properly recognised, was the first Livingston Community Council that had John Ross for its Chairperson and Jim Law as its Secretary. In my view, the real significance of this development lay not so much in the business dealt with, but in the very fact of its existence. Here was a body that saw itself as being there for the town as a whole, to give voice to its concerns and to give a sense of corporate identity to the people themselves.

The reorganisation of local government brought in from Lord Wheatley's proposals gave us local Community Councils throughout the town, but nothing to allow us make common cause on town-wide concerns. This serious omission is still there and one can only hope that, with the new local government structures now being put in place and the wind-up in 1996 of the Development Corporation itself, this civic blank will be dealt with and some kind of democratically elected Council be set up.

PART TWO
Working at it Together

I praise you, Father,
Lord of heaven and earth,
because you have hidden these things
from the wise and learned
and revealed them to little children

Luke 10: 21
(New International Version)

CHAPTER 5

Team Ministry

FROM the beginning the Team Ministry has been the corner-stone of the Churches' work in Livingston. No Church authority ever decided that there should be a Team Ministry for the co-operating denominations. This was a decision made by the people on the ground, the assumption being that this was the obvious way to work and that anything else could only be an impossible mismatch.

The Team was there to give meaning and support to the work of ministry throughout the parish. It exercised no authority over the Churches. That authority must always lie, and be seen to lie, with the Churches themselves. We never had a team leader as such, but always a chairperson appointed for one year.

The strength of the Team way of working came, in the main, from the regular weekly meeting, and the quality of sharing it stimulated and encouraged. Someone who had to plough a lone furrow in his/her ministry for many years, could and did find a release of fresh confidence and energy through the discovery that we really are in this together and can be of genuine help to one another in good times and bad. For people in full-time professional ministry, membership of a lively and committed team of men and women can do so much to provide the wherewithal 'to meet with triumph and disaster and to treat these two impostors just the same'.

It was the Team Ministry in Livingston that brought home to me the basic importance of the so-called lay people and how the main work of 'the full-time professionals' must be to inspire and equip the people themselves to fulfil their all-important role in the Lord's mission of love to the world.

> *Christ has no body now on earth but yours,*
> *no hands but yours,*
> *no feet but yours.*

Yours are the eyes through which he is to look out
Christ's compassion to the world;
Yours are the feet with which he is to go about doing good;
Yours are the hands with which he is to bless men now.

~ Saint Teresa of Avila ~

You – the people, the ministers, the priests – you are the body of Christ.

Friendly critics would sometimes suggest that for a team like ours, with no team tradition or model to work from, and with little or no experience of the team way of working, there are two besetting dangers.

One is that we are overtaken by the 'three brass monkeys syndrome' – 'See no evil. Hear no evil. Speak no evil.'

True, life is easier this way. No one is upset, no one ever troubled or put out. But how utterly unreal and defeating such practice would be, however appealing it might sound especially at the beginning when we all felt quite unsure of ourselves. This 'three brass monkeys syndrome', it should be said, was never a temptation for any of us once the team began to function properly.

The other danger was quite the opposite and took an almost totalitarian view of team and teampersonship – *ie* 'Nothing against the team, nothing outwith the team, nothing but what the team approves for its members and their working life.' This, if rigidly followed, could be stultifying and terribly inhibiting of personal, group, congregational initiative, and that could mean nothing but death to the Spirit's working.

The Team Ministry had, for us all, one main purpose – to strengthen one another's hands for the work of furthering the unity of God's people in our own locality and throughout the world. We tried to do this in three main ways – By sharing concern for:

–   The life of the Community.
–   The life of the Churches.
–   The needs of our World.

The Life of the Community

As readers know, the original team was made up of three ministers and one lay member. With such a make-up, you might expect team-thinking and discussing to be clerical from first to last. That this was not so was, for most part, due to the forcefulness of the lay member, Max Cruickshank – to the liveliness of his mind, the vigour and forthrightness of his speaking, as well as to the all-pervading strength of his feeling for people whatever their social, financial or religious standing.

Craigs Farm

Because Max was as much a community worker as a youth worker, he saw to it that a big part of every team meeting was devoted to the needs, immediate and long term, of the families all around us. This would be in their relations to one another and to the town itself, now expanding at such a rate that many residents, especially young mothers, could easily feel left out and lost. Max was as enthusiastic as any about the New Town Forum on Sunday mornings and did more than most to give it sparkle and appeal. He was also mainly instrumental in persuading his own Church, the Church of Scotland, to put up the money, some hundreds of pounds, so that the old Craigs Farm buildings could be taken over by the churches in the Ecumenical Parish and developed as a centre, as a natural meeting place for the people of Craigshill.

By dint of patience and remarkable stick-ability, Max succeeded in persuading sufficient volunteers to bring their skill and time and labour to convert the old farmhouse kitchen into a cafe and to have it functioning in a matter of months.

Here, ahead of the new pub – how we envied the speed and ease with which the brewers' people went about their business! – here were the beginnings of a community project that over the years has contributed immeasurably to the sense of belonging amongst young and old in Craigshill.

Once the reconstruction work on the old kitchen had been completed, the other parts of the original farmhouse had to be made usable. Here again the Church of Scotland gave great help through one of its Home Board architects. Young people of the churches locally, as well as from Edinburgh, Musselburgh and elsewhere, weighed in with us in different weekend working parties. The Quest Group of Greenbank Church, Edinburgh made a quite outstanding contribution by working with us for two entire holiday weeks. All these young people worked hard, but they also enjoyed themselves and greatly helped to spread a spirit of cheerful purposefulness throughout the area.

Livingston owes more to the Churches than it will ever realise. What was so impressive for many of us about Max and these church youth groups was the reality of their faith – that what they were engaged in at Craigs Farm was nothing less than a reaching out to that Kingdom that has room enough in it for the hurt, the broken and the vulnerable, as well as for the gifted and well-resourced.

How often I find myself wishing that now, after almost thirty years, these young people could come back and see for themselves this 'centre of excellence' that is Craigs Farm today! I like to think that they would detect, as I often do, about all that is happening here – in the cafe with its banter and warmth, the political meetings, the Justice and Peace activities, the young folks' music making, in the many different groups for which the Farm is home – that in and about them all is a resonance of caring and hopefulness that 'the best is yet to be' for them, for Craigshill, for Livingston. If, in some very limited sense, the three ministers in the team were the voice of the Church in Scotland, then Max was the voice of the people. To have such a voice at team meetings and elsewhere was of quite inestimable, if sometimes disquieting, worth.

Take one example – Max argued strongly that, from the point of view of community renewal, the Churches' youth work was so fragmented that it could do little or nothing to help young people realise that they are meant to belong together in active, recognisable solidarity. The uniformed organisations were doing excellent training work, but they were doing it separately and often in competition with each other. Max pleaded with the local youth leaders for their members to be allowed to come together on one evening per week, to follow quite strictly a programme of joint training for the first hour and then fun and games for the second. This did take place and ran successfully enough for the best part of a year. It had to be wound up because a majority of the organisational leaders felt that the distinctive contribution of the different organisations was being lost entirely.

That this 'teaming up' did take place, and was shared by so many, was an achievement that few outside Livingston would have believed possible. Who can say what the long-term consequences of such an experience could be for these youngsters? It was bound to make them readier to recognise the undoubted benefits that flow from learning how to come together and stay together. There is, of course, such a thing as friendly rivalry, but who could deny that Scottish life and culture, not to say religion, have suffered far too much already from rivalries that are anything but friendly?

It was this disturbing 'voice of the people' that kept us ministers constantly aware of the growing chasm between church and people. A telling, if quite hurtful, instance of this occurred when Max was centering his youth work on the Craigs Farm Project. Very strongly he pleaded with the minister members of the Team: 'Please don't come near the Farm just now. If these teenagers see ministers coming around they'll conclude that this is really a Church project and that would ruin everything!'

Let none imagine that in the search for a truer community life the ministers were mere passengers. The ministers – and Father John Byrne – were in the thick of things at Forum every Sunday morning. All of us were united and strongly believed that the shaping of the new town's corporate life, the unremitting effort to enrich its quality and strengthen its inclusiveness, had to be top priority for us all as congregations and individuals.

Lanthorn

We have already seen how Hamish Smith and then his successor, Ross McLaren, succeeded, with the backing and co-operation of the different local authorities, in setting up the Lanthorn Centre in Dedridge. Shortly after its opening, there was a BBC radio broadcast describing Lanthorn and telling how it came to be. Of all the letters and phone calls we received as a result of that broadcast, the one I remember most thankfully was that from the world-famous Scots journalist James Cameron in London. In his column in *The*

Guardian he told how he had listened to the broadcast in delighted surprise and said that it had done more to lift his spirits than anything else he had heard all week.

The heady days at Lanthorn were the early years when Ross McLaren was manager of the place, Revd Joan Ryeland (Methodist) was in charge of the ecumenical ministry there, and the new priests were young and eager to co-operate. Now, some twenty years later, people in Dedridge still speak very warmly of Joan, of her liveliness and freshness in her church work and, especially, of the unsparing way she spent herself in the work of Dedridge Community Council. It is still true, in Livingston as elsewhere, that however good the physical provision may be for community life and church life, it is still the reality of personal commitment and the readiness 'to labour and not to ask for any reward' that the Spirit blesses and empowers.

Joan was the first woman member of our Team Ministry and a very valuable member she proved to be. Partly as a result of her many years experience in the Methodist Diaconate, she was able to bring a width of understanding to our discussions, as well as a freshness and terseness to our shared prayers. Most important of all, by her very presence in the team, Joan was able to give us an increasing awareness of the male chauvinism that quite unconsciously pervaded, and sometimes dominated, much of our thinking and planning.

Everyone in the Livingston Ecumenical Parish had reason for special thankfulness to our Diocesan Bishop, Alastair Haggart, for so readily agreeing to Joan having the same freedom as the other ministers in the Livingston Team – to preside at Communion celebrations according to the order followed by the Scottish Episcopal Church. This was a significant breakthrough for ministry in Scotland, and one that should be noted not just for the record but for a truer appreciation of the reality of ecumenical advance in the thinking of Scottish Church leaders.

The Life of the Churches – Concerns

Archbishop William Temple once wrote:

Because we pride ourselves on being a practical people, we are liable to say that conduct is the really important thing and that prayer is very valuable because it helps conduct. But if God is the most real thing in the world, that puts it wrong; and the right way to put it is that prayer is the most important thing in life and conduct tests it.

He went on to say:

The most effective thing that the Church of Christ can do in this world, and the most effective thing that any Christian can do, is to lift up his/her heart in adoration to God .... Adoration, the utter giving of the self to God that he might fill it, a total forgetfulness of self in the presence of God that he may be all in all – that is the heart of worship.

To gain this experience of worship, to be caught up in the feeling for the 'real presence' that William Temple is talking about, is not something that large numbers of people find happening to them in the routine services we share in any of our mainline churches these days. Does not the great appeal of Iona and its abbey worship lie in the power of that worship in that place to release people into this kind of self-forgetting prayer, praise and adoration – especially, perhaps, in the service of Holy Communion on Sunday mornings?

'To taste and see' all this for ourselves can be wonderful beyond words, but it has its obvious dangers. One such danger is that, for some, God is alive on Iona, but not, or not in the same soul-quickening way, in the local church back home. What can be done about this?

Some would say that nothing short of a Spirit-led renewal of life in our local churches and communities will do. While praying for this kind of renewal, something that could be regarded as ongoing preparation for it was made accessible to us in the Livingston ecumenical experience of worship. This, in my view, is bound up with the kind of glorying in God that the Apostles and the saints – and William Temple – make so much of.

Church of Scotland people, Congregationalists and Methodists, are all at home in services of worship that are much the same in all three traditions. For those born and bred into any one of these traditions, to feel comfortable and confident with the carefully-worded, carefully-structured liturgical service is so demanding that very few are prepared to make the effort required. This, as I see it now, is to our own spiritual impoverishment.

Part of the significance of the Livingston ecumenical commitment lies in the fact that all the churches of the Ecumenical Parish have on offer two kinds of corporate worship available every Sunday morning – the more freely ordered service centering on the Word; but also the fully responsive liturgical service centering on the Eucharist. As one who spent more than half his ministry leading Church of Scotland services, and who never imagined that anything different could ever match this particular way of waiting on the Lord and worshipping together, I have to say that the effort demanded by trying to get properly into this liturgical way of worshipping is eminently worthwhile and an effort that every committed believer should be encouraged to make.

Brian Hardy

We were particularly fortunate in these critical, formative years in the person who was the Episcopal member of the Team Ministry – Brian Hardy. He had a gentle persuasiveness about him, such an instinctive feeling for the Gospel, and such a depth of personal spirituality that those of us in the non-Episcopal traditions were able to learn very quickly through him how meaningful, real and uplifting liturgical worship can be. A very great asset to him and to us in all of this was Brian's gift for music, whereby he was able to help us learn and enjoy many new songs. The one I best remember had this chorus:

When I fall on my knees
with my face to the rising sun,
O Lord have mercy on me.

Far and away the most important feature of the 9.30 Episcopal Service was the Holy Communion always at the heart of it. What a privilege it was for us ministers sometimes to preside, sometimes to assist, sometimes to be a member of the worshipping congregation! How good it would be if, in all our churches, the life of the congregation could be so ordered that one person, the minister, would not need always to be in charge, always to be 'holding forth'!

All of us in the original Team Ministry would, I am sure, agree that being able to share in the main services of worship – especially in the communion as a member of the congregation – was of the greatest benefit to each of us in all kinds of ways. Perhaps the most salutary lesson was the way in which this practice helped us realise how easy it can be for the worshippers, or at least some of them, to feel lost and left behind, even in an Episcopal service where vocal participation by the people is at a maximum.

Brian was able to gather a group of 15 or so teenage boys and had them singing some very new (to us) and very lovely songs at the 9.30 Communion on Sunday mornings. This created quite a stir of interest and brought many new people to take part in this service. For a period there were more Church of Scotland and Congregationalist and Methodist members than Episcopalians sharing and greatly enjoying the worship at 9.30. Active participation through the responsive prayers, and perhaps still more the very personal way of receiving Communion, had a great deal to do with the appeal of this particular service, a service that has its roots in the ancient liturgies of the Church through the ages.

There can be few more urgent challenges to the church people of Scotland than that so willingly taken up by Brian Hardy in the first committed venturing on the part of the Churches here towards a new life together for Jesus' sake and for the good of the country and all its people. We have to pray then that more opportunities will be forthcoming for other Brian Hardys to open up in real and loving ways the shining truth the Lord is waiting to reveal as we find one another in the healing peace of his Spirit.

Learning how

At St Columba's, part of the first communicants' training for full church membership consisted of at least two attendances at the 9.30 Episcopal Communion. In discussing the service at later class meetings, the young people would say something like this:

We were put off at the beginning by the use of the prayer book and trying to follow the prayers so that we were joining in at the right places. Before the end of the service, however, we were beginning to get the hang of it. Our attendance on the following Sunday was a much better experience. We see the point of not just listening – or not listening – to one person out there praying but saying out the words ourselves.

Seeing people going forward – several of them in family groups – and then kneeling to receive the bread and wine with the word spoken to each one, 'The Body of Christ', 'The Blood of Christ' – all this must and does help participants feel that this is for real, that they are being personally and particularly addressed and drawn afresh into God's amazing grace. One family at St Columba's, both parents elders in the Church of Scotland, found it suited them to worship with their two children at the 9.30 Communion. That this way of making their Communion as individuals and as a family made a deep impression on the children is borne out by the parents. One of them has told how they were all sitting round the table waiting to start their midday meal with soup, when the older child leaned forward, picked up a quarter slice of bread from the plate at the centre of the table, then turned to her father. Holding out the bread to him, the child said, 'Body of Christ, Daddy'. How powerfully a simple incident like this brings the Lord's words into mind:

Let the children come to me … for the Kingdom of God belongs to such as these. I tell you, whoever does not accept the the Kingdom of God like a child will never enter it.

~ Mark 10: 14, 15 ~

Here is the child sensing, and saying, that to share in the Sacrament of Communion is to see something of the Sacrament in every common meal. When some such awareness as this takes proper hold on us, we can be sure that in all our meals at home, in the work canteen, in the cafe, 'the real presence' is there as well.

How much poorer this family's life would have been, how much poorer the lives of many of us in Livingston would have been, if our regular Sunday worship had been restricted to the one denominational pattern and practice.

Bangour Village Hospital

One very real benefit of the Team Ministry way of working lay in being able to allocate certain areas of work to different members of the Team. Under this arrangement it was decided that my own part in hospital visitation should be Bangour Village Hospital for people suffering from mental and nervous disorder, and also the place where those suffering from troubles that come in old age are cared for.

Because I did not have to go rushing on to see patients in other hospitals, I could spend one afternoon per week, sometimes two, seeing people whose homes were in Livingston. Then, at the next Team Meeting, I could pass on such information as mattered to their own minister in the Ecumenical Parish for him/her to share with the family.

I am not at all sure that my ministry in this needy area counted for as much as it could have done, but certainly the men, women and young people I was privileged to meet in this hospital context made me realise how important the Church's pastoral involvement can be both for the Church and for the sufferers themselves.

I had to learn a far greater humility. Quite often at the sight of my 'dog collar', a patient would just clam up, saying without words: 'You have nothing for me and I have nothing to say to you.' Next time round it could be the same, but usually by the third approach some kind of communication could begin. That communication had to be two-way, but primarily my role, as I saw it, was one of listening, learning, receiving and then offering it in prayer there, perhaps, and certainly later. Sensitivity is all, sensitivity to the person beside me, but also sensitivity to the Spirit's own prompting out of the story he or she was telling. It was this particular awareness that allowed any prayers we said together to have meaning, and at least the promise of healing, and the sense, perhaps a growing sense, of a strong helper at work within.

It made all the difference if the people I was seeing and trying to pray with were being prayed for by name (first name only) by the people of the congregations. Without this being given a significant place in the congregation's continuing intercession, the effectiveness of the pastoral work being attempted could be cut by half.

As I went about the hospital's different wards, I came to feel increasingly uneasy about people suffering from dementia of one kind or another in so many long-stay wards for whom neither I nor anyone else seemed to be doing anything at all. They were being cared for devotedly enough by sister, nurses, orderlies and, of course, the doctors, but beyond that hardly anyone seemed to be bothering to make contact or show any kind of personal interest.

I happened to know one of the ward sisters whose home was in Craigshill and I talked with her about her own ward and the possibility of holding a Sing-along Service with her patients some Sunday afternoon. She couldn't have been more positive or co-operative. So a group from different churches in Livingston, singers and guitar players, agreed to give one Sunday afternoon in every four weeks to providing a simple and very lighthearted service of singing, praying and celebrating the Lord's loving, life-renewing presence. What pleased us all so much was that sister, nurses, orderlies took an enthusiastic part in every service and helped the patients take their part as well.

It was indeed a learning and deeply moving experience to see again and again a person who could not remember so much as her own name, singing a line or two from a hymn she had learned in childhood such as 'Jesus loves me this I know'.

If it is true that the real source of health and wholeness for any people lies not so much with the medical professionals as with the local congregations of the Lord's freed-up and caring people, then every congregation with its ministers and priests has to face the question – are we doing all we could to allow the Lord's life-giving Spirit to be shared more freely amongst ourselves and with those who are in weakness and infirmity and growing dependence? These are the very people who undoubtedly rank first in the Gospel's scale of priorities.

Mother Teresa of Calcutta has a prayer that goes something like this:

Make us worthy Lord to serve our fellow men and women throughout the world who live and die in great need and lostness.
Give them through our hands this day their daily bread and by our understanding give peace and joy.

The Needs of the World – the Global Village

Protestant churchmanship in twentieth century Scotland has the reputation of being strongly isolationist and so often seems to pay little attention to what is happening in church life in other parts of the United Kingdom and the wider world. However strong the temptation for us in the Team Ministry to indulge this kind of outlook, we would never have been allowed to get away with it for very long.

One of our team came from south of the border with a wide experience of the Church of England at parish level and at university level. That in itself did much to prevent the parochial mind taking over. And with a person like Robert Mackie in close and constant contact with all of us in the Team, we could hardly avoid being kept aware of the World Council of Churches and its increasing concern for refugees, apartheid in South Africa, and all that was going on, with World Council backing, to combat racism in so many countries.

The World Council's Theological College at Bossey, Switzerland was generous enough to arrange for a minister member of one of their main ecumenical training courses to spend three months with us in Livingston, sharing the experience of a grassroots experiment and taking a full part in the Team Ministry's discussions and work with church and community. Under this arrangement we had men from places like the Philippines, Canada and Sierra Leone. These visitors did a great deal to give us and the congregations a fresh glimpse of the everyday life of people in another country, as well as a pulsing 'sough' of the Spirit in the ways and worship of the Churches there. This proved a most valuable service and one that we all appreciated at the time and appreciate still more in retrospect.

A young minister, Sam Prempeh, from the Presbyterian Church in Ghana, spent a year with us in 1972-73. Under the auspices of the Church of Scotland, he was doing a post-graduate course at New College, Edinburgh University's Theological Faculty. He brought a gladness and colourfulness into our life and worship, and made us realise how much we had to gain from maintaining a living relationship with church and people in this 'Third World' country. Some of us had still to learn of another need in our relationships with Ghana and other African countries – the need to find ways of making real repentance for our part in the slave trade that had inflicted such suffering, degradation and blight on the lives of millions in Africa.

In his book *Unfinished Agenda* (Saint Andrew Press, 1994), Lesslie Newbigin writes of his visit to Ghana:

> *More than anything else I shall remember the visit to the old English fort at Cape Coast, where the African slaves were kept chained in a dark dungeon at water level till the boats took them to the slave ships, while in the chapel immediately above, the English garrison conducted worship, keeping watch through a hole in the floor on the inmates of the dungeon below. I am always amazed that these crimes can be so easily forgotten. Ever since that visit I have wished that some representative Englishman – an archbishop or a prime minister – might come to Ghana and go down to that dungeon, kneel down on the floor and offer a prayer of contrition. I still hope it may happen.*

For an archbishop or a prime minister to give open verbal expression before God and the African people to penitence and sorrow for our part in the evil of slavery, could be of far-reaching spiritual and social significance. But signs must follow such a gesture.

A famous German theologian, Johann Baptiste Metz, wrote that it is no longer possible to do theology with one's back turned to Auschwitz. This is well said, but is it not equally true that it is no longer permissible for us to do, or *try* to do, theology with our back turned on Ghana and the other African countries which were made to suffer so terribly by the enslaving countries of Europe and America?

Are the Churches now being called to recognise that behind Auschwitz, behind slavery, lies a deeper dereliction of faith? Does this same age-old dereliction help to explain our heart-breaking failure to prevent the resurgence of racism in central Europe with its 'ethnic cleansing', or the increase in our own country of ever-deepening social dividedness, or worse – the 'silent holocaust' in Third World countries as hunger and poverty wreak havoc amongst them and millions of children abandoned to the streets of the city?

For hundreds of years now, we have regarded it as quite permissible to sing the Lord's songs, to pray his prayer, to share his communion while insisting on maintaining our separate and distinct identities. This, in my view, is the sin at back of all the others, the purblind persistence in wrong-doing that sets a kind of poisoned chalice at the heart of all our words and works. To allow a deep-going change of heart and outlook to come about within us and through us, we are being called out of our exclusive groupings and denominations to be quite simply the two or three meeting together in the name of nothing else, of no one else but the Lord Christ, the crucified and risen One. To start all over again with one another and with him who made himself of no reputation, who took upon himself the form of a slave, must mean allowing ourselves to be drawn into the Lord's passion and prayer as he faces his continuing Gethsemane, betrayal, humiliation and death. We become participants in the mystery of the Gospel, in a love-renewing, reconciling power when, as one writer has put it: 'we are so challenged by something beyond our own achievement that we cannot help responding, repenting, turning, moving and being moved.'

The Livingston experience matters for Scotland because there are people in this town who can testify to the following: that even a limited but actual everyday commitment to a more united and open way of being God's people allows something of new community joy and purpose to happen, and to happen in such a way that those touched by it find stirring within them a new feeling for the neighbours around, for God's world and for all his creatures.

Now, in union with Christ Jesus, you who used to be far away have been brought near by the death of Christ. For Christ himself has brought us peace, by making Jews and Gentiles one people. With his own body he broke down the wall that separated them and kept them enemies .... By his death on the cross Christ destroyed the hatred and by means of that cross he united both races into one single body and brought them back to God. ~ Ephesians 2: 13-16 (Good News Bible) ~

India

For all of us in the Team Ministry, India stood out as the country of special promise and challenge. This was not just because India was the country of Mahatma Gandhi, and of Christians of quite remarkable courage and saintliness such as Sadhu Sundar Singh, but because it is the country where the first ecumenically significant union of the Churches took place in 1947. The United Church of South India that came into being then is made up of Anglicans and British Methodists who joined up with an already united body of Congregationalists and Presbyterians, making this union the first of its kind in the world. Twenty-three years later, the Church of North India, with a still wider grouping, came into being. So there was an eagerness amongst us to learn all we could from this great country and its ecumenical pioneers. Three sets of people were of particular help to us in this regard

The first was John Macleod, his wife Sheila, and their family. The second was Tom Kunenkeril, his wife and family. The third was Bhailal Patel, his wife Sharda and all their children.

The Macleods

The Macleod family, and one or two of their friends, formed a little orchestra to lead Sunday morning's praise in the Carmondean centre. Songs with new tunes were very much to the fore. People in the congregation were never left for long 'just sitting there'. Active participation by children, young people and older members was taken as a must at almost every service. 'Nothing can be taught; everything can be learned' seemed to be the watchword both at St Paul's and then at Carmondean, and everyone was expected to contribute to the loving atmosphere that makes real learning possible.

Perhaps the greatest of the gifts they brought us from their time in India was their own strong awareness of the all-pervading, all-encompassing love of God for all his children – Hindu, Muslim, Christian – as well as those who counted themselves amongst the irreligious. Both John and Sheila felt quite strongly that the Welfare State in Britain had somehow lost its way; that essentially secular attitudes were prevailing everywhere, even in the Churches; that we no longer accepted personal responsibility for the neighbour God has given us as one not only to be served in the sharing of material benefits, but also to be loved, to be prayed for, and to be prayed with and given a sense of his/her own distinctive and irreplaceable part in the family and the purposes of God.

Tom Kunenkeril

Tom Kunenkeril was a member of the Church of Scotland's Faith Share Team that operated throughout the country for a period of three months in 1973. He was allocated to Livingston for one week – and what a stimulating time this was for us at the manse and for the different people who had the chance of listening to him and meeting him at the many gatherings where he was telling the story of the Gospel and its impact on the life and people of Kerala in South India!

Tom had spent his working life in the Indian Navy and his last posting, just prior to retirement, had been as his country's Naval Attache to the Indian Embassy in Berlin. Clearly he was no slouch, nor yet a cold civil service type, but exuded a genial self-forgetting humility, a sparkling sense of humour, as well as an insatiable interest in the people he was meeting.

Three things in Tom's life we found particularly impressive. First, he rose every morning at five o'clock. Second, he spent the first hour in prayer and meditation (part of that meditation he called Christian Yoga). Third, the next hour he spent writing to his wife at home in Kerala. She couldn't be with him, but she had to be told of everything that was happening to and around her husband.

The highlight of this Faith Share week in Livingston was without question his visits to Craigshill High School, where the pupils, usually so restive and switched-off at morning assembly, were hanging on his every word.

He spoke about young people in his part of India. He told how his own son had been caught up in the drug scene, how he was taken seriously ill and his life despaired of. While he was lying unconscious in hospital, his mother would spend the day and a good part of every night at his bedside. But she wasn't just looking at him and holding his hand. She kept speaking to him. She kept praying for him. She kept saying out loud some of the death-defying words of Scripture like: 'Jesus said ... Jesus says, "I am the good shepherd. The good shepherd gives his life for the sheep".'

His son did recover and became a Christian believer. He sent with his father a tape-recording, giving his own account of the hammering he had taken from his abuse of drugs, and also his personal testimony to the life-saving power of the Gospel.

'I would like all the young people of Scotland to hear it,' were his parting words to his father as he set out on Operation Faith Share. One High School pupil spoke of the effect that tape-recording had on her, saying, 'I never heard anything so telling, so moving'.

On the morning of Tom's departure, he said goodbye, pushed his bags into the waiting car and was suddenly stopped in his tracks. He came running back into the sitting room to say: 'Look! When I was telling you about Christian Yoga, I promised to let you see my standing on the head exercise. Here it is …'. There and then this man of God, this man of the Spirit, stood on his head so easily, so gracefully – and smiling all the while.

I remember mentioning this to a group of ministers, one of whom volunteered the suggestion that this might be made a test of suitability for the job of Moderator of the General Assembly of the Church of Scotland: 'Can he stand on his head? Easily? Gracefully? … and smiling all the while?'

The Patels

Sharda and Bhailal Patel came to Livingston with their family at the beginning of the new town, when the Forum influence was at its strongest. Prior to this they had been living in London and found life there cold and unwelcoming after the close knit community that had been their's in India. To find, as they did in Livingston, that neighbours were welcoming and helpful, did much to dispel the feelings of being aliens and strangers, feelings that can be such a seed-bed of resentment, anger, fear ….

Bhailal was an architect with the Livingston Development Corporation. He was full of enthusiasm not only for working with his brother/sister architects to give 'a human face' to the new districts and the town centre itself as these were beginning to emerge, but also for the famous town planners of Scotland who had blazed such a promising trail of 'better building for better community'. The new buildings, by their design and lay-out, would be helping to give the people in them, and coming around them, a stronger sense of their own dignity and worth. Chief of these famous architects and town planners, certainly for Bhailal, was Patrick Geddes of Edinburgh. Bhailal himself could never understand how the civic authorities in Scotland seemed to have bypassed so much of this kind of 'forward planning' and allowed these vast and soul-less housing areas to become such a bleak and dreary feature of Scotland's civic life. 'It is these,' he would say, 'that cannot but breed amongst their residents a degenerating sense of their nobodiness.'

The Patels were not only at home amongst us. By their friendliness and readiness to co-operate, they made their own positive contribution to the good-neighbourliness and sense of purpose of the place. In any move for the betterment of life in Livingston, Bhailal could be counted on to pull his weight and to encourage others to do the same. He took a leading part in the move to prevent the Bopal Company with all its proven dangers from setting up in Livingston. He worked very hard with Councillor Revd Ross McLaren and others to have the first and badly needed railway station built in Livingston – 'Livingston South' – giving another access to Edinburgh in the east, to Glasgow in the west, and to many small towns and villages in between.

Of all the good works Bhailal was involved in, the one that impressed us the most was his heading up of the appeal to provide immediate succour to people in Bangladesh suffering so terribly from a recent disaster. Bangladesh is a Muslim country and everyone knows of the age-old hostility between Muslim and Hindu. The Patels were a loyal and deeply devout Hindu family, but this did not prevent Bhailal, his wife and children, working day and night to provide immediate and practical help. Some of us were reminded of the words of Jesus: 'If your enemy hunger, feed him', and also of the ways and urgings of Gandhi, an Indian prophet and more than a prophet of the Kingdom of God.

All of us in the Team Ministry, all of us in the Churches of Livingston, can never be grateful enough for the enhancement of life and religion brought to us directly and indirectly by India and so many of its spiritually-minded people.

CHAPTER 6

Children and Young People

M Y first contact with the children of the New Town happened early in May 1966 when I visited the newly-opened Riverside Primary School in Craigshill. Nicol Kerr was the Head and sole teacher in the school which, at that point, had only six pupils. Mr Kerr was unable to greet me with the customary handshake because the youngest child in the school, not yet five, had grown tired, climbed up on the Head Teacher's knee and fallen sound asleep. On my return home to Airdrie, I can remember saying to Elizabeth that I hoped every Head appointed to the many new schools planned for Livingston would be the kind of person on to whose knees a very young child could instinctively climb to rest and sleep.

The New Town Forum's concern for education was continued long after Forum's day. The Convener of Midlothian's Education Committee, Willie Rankine of West Calder, came again and again to meet the people and answer their questions. There were times when he took a lot of flak, but he never turned nasty and he never gave up on us. This was one of the serious losses that occurred with the advent of the Lothian Regional Council taking full responsibility for education throughout the Lothians including the city of Edinburgh. The regional area is so wide and the number of children, parents and teachers so large, that the Education Committee with its Convener became for most people faceless and remote. Some very good work was done for Livingston by this Committee – an outstanding example of which was the initiation and development of Community High Schools. But the facelessness remained.

The then Director of Education for Midlothian, Tom Henderson, visited Livingston two or three times on a Sunday morning in the first two years. He always had much to say on the Committee's plans for the area and made a great deal of their policy for building not just a straight primary school, but a school plus a Youth/Community wing. This particular provision was much appreciated, but it had its limitations and came in for some serious criticism. It was socially healthy, perhaps, that the Director himself was hearing these – and other – negative comments, not at second hand from his officials or even Committee members, but 'straight from the horse's mouth'.

I like to think that these discussions with the Convener and the Director contributed a little to the willingness of the different local authorities to consider a radically different centre for the community in the Dedridge area.

The Numbers Game

It soon became apparent that schools in Livingston, like schools in all the large towns and cities, were contending with the fiercely intractable problem of numbers. A stable, long-established community can perhaps find ways of coping, but in all the rawness and lack of social cohesion that characterise large new communities this is virtually impossible. Given proper motivation on the part of parents and children, thirty pupils or more are manageable, teachable, as the record in so many African countries can testify. When this kind of motivation is missing, then classes in the upper twenties make the kind of learning the good teacher wants to encourage quite impossible. The price of failure here has often to be paid later on in secondary school, where teachers of third and fourth year students are faced with the herculean task of trying to build where foundations have never been properly laid. The truth is that the full price of failure in the primary classes is paid by the children themselves throughout their lives. It is costly to them and to us all.

Smaller classes must never be regarded as a panacea for all our educational ills. In inner cities however, in new towns and most of all in the harsh inhumanity of our peripheral housing areas, the creative possibilities latent in the real, living relationships between a group of, say, twelve children and a fully trained, caring and responsible adult, can be life-transforming for pupils and teacher alike.

If we are serious about the remaking of our society along fairer, more just, more inclusive lines, then the first thing we have all to accept is a much, much bigger financial outlay on educating our children and young people.

William Faulkner, the famous prophetic American writer, says: 'Some things you must always be unable to bear. Some things you must never stop refusing to bear – injustice and outrage, dishonour and shame.'

The time has surely come for many more people in Scotland to rouse themselves and to raise their voices against the injustice and outrage, the dishonour and shame of contentedly consigning the education of our children to the bargain basement of social provision. Thinking to have education on the cheap is criminal in itself and cannot but make for criminality throughout the community.

Direct Involvement

We were so fortunate in Livingston that the Church of Scotland's full time Youth Worker was Max Cruickshank. He was able, as few others were, to make contact with the teenagers and young adults, to gain their confidence and build up real and trusting relationships.

Max insisted on working in close partnership with the County Council's Youth Leader, Jack Nixon. Together they saw to it that the young folk were never left to spend their evenings or their weekends in boredom. As well as the usual club activities, these youngsters were given the chance of taking part in all kinds of outings – hill-walking, ski-ing, canoeing, rock-climbing. They were also encouraged to contribute to the life of their own community by joining a work party renovating the old Craigs Farm buildings. Two things further are perhaps worth adding.

When young people landed themselves in trouble with the police, the first person they turned to was Max. He never let them off with a smack on the wrist. Later, when Max had moved from Livingston to East Kilbride, it was a member of the police force who said: 'Max's departure is going to make our work ten times harder.'

The other thing you could be sure of with Max was that although a Church Youth Worker, he would never be heard saying to any young person, 'come to church'.

While this way of working with present-day youth was understandable and directly in line with the Ecumenical Parish's constant stress on the Church's need to be concerned with people as people and not just as potential pew-fillers, I used to think that Max and the rest of us might have taken more pains to help new town residents, including the young people, to realise that in Livingston a new kind of Church was struggling to be born. This newness had to do with more than ecumenical co-operation as conventionally understood. Rather, it had to do with a new kind of openness to the community and its people, a readiness to be involved with so-called secular enterprise and a clear rejection of 'triumphalism' in its many different guises. In other words, in struggling to be 'salt', 'leaven', and even 'light', we had to work hard at helping one another to see and keep seeing the spiritual centre of gravity not within the congregations, but out there in the life of the surrounding locality with all its aspirations, frustrations and dead-ends.

Families

Chris Reid was the first District Nurse in the new town. In any community, the District Nurse and Health Visitor have vitally important roles to play. They are dealing directly with people at their point of need and most particularly with young mothers who often 'have it all to learn' and can feel very vulnerable and deeply lacking in confidence.

Chris, by her make-up as a person, by her training, outlook and feeling for people, was able to communicate simply and directly the considerable know-how necessary for coping with the new baby and the new family situation that the new baby brings about. More than that, because of her belief in the new town itself, because of her personal involvement in the ecumenical development of the new Church and its way of working, she was able to impart something of a 'feel-good' element to mothers and their children, and quite often to young fathers as well. The almost unconscious ability to do this does more for personal and family morale than most of us could ever realise.

Chris, with Pat Cruikshank, was responsible for bringing the social psychologist, Max Paterson, to meet and talk with the Play Groups that did so much to pioneer the way for nursery schooling that is now generally accepted as a basic provision for every child.

One specially significant contribution to the common good made by Chris Reid in these early years came through her willingness to run the creche for young children on Sunday mornings. With a group of helpers, she did this Sunday after Sunday from before 10.30 until after 12.30. This provision made it possible for mothers and fathers to take part in Forum and/or in one or other of the 11.30 Services of Worship. It is important to recognise that this was far more then a babyminding arrangement. It was a service to families and to the community lovingly and responsibly given. Without it, the feeling of social warmth amongst us all would never have attained the reality and strength it did.

Sunday School

By the end of 1966 families were beginning to flood into Craigshill. There was little on offer for these families beyond the basic necessities of house, school, grocer and doctor's surgery – little, that is, except a welcoming neighbourliness and a readiness to be helpful in every practical way. Because this sense of togetherness was so palpable amongst us, the job of setting up a Sunday School for children of all ages proved exciting and highly encouraging.

Sheila Moyes of the Church of Scotland's Youth Committee gave quite invaluable help in the initial stages. Before long children, quite literally in their hundreds, were taking part in our Sunday morning activities – all of which were centred on the Riverside Primary School, its classrooms and main hall. Not only were the children attending in large numbers, but adults were eagerly offering their help.

The Sunday morning pattern was of the simplest. There were three departments – Primary, Juniors and Seniors – meeting in different classrooms from 11.30. At 12.15 one department per Sunday joined the adult congregation and shared with the congregation something of the work they'd been doing, the lessons they were learning, on that and earlier Sunday mornings. As I remember, the biggest influence on our work with children came from H. A. Hamilton of the Congregational Church in England and his pioneering of the Family Church.

Hamilton had one dominating principle – 'Not a child in the school without a friend in the church' – and this build-up of close relationships between the children and the adult congregation imparted a strange quickening power to the work of the Sunday School and the life of the congregation.

We were trying to work along the same lines with one quite radical difference. Instead of 'Not a child in the church without a friend in the church', we had 'Not a child in the parish without a friend in the church'. For the years 1967 and '68 this way of working seemed to be productive in terms of good results, especially among the young children. Then, in 1969, we had to move from Riverside School to the new building, St Columba's – and this started us on a quite different 'ball game'.

Only the Primary Department could be housed at St Columba's on a Sunday morning. The other two departments and the Bible Class had to continue meeting in Riverside School. To try to bridge the gap between children and congregation, we started a monthly Family Service geared to children and younger people with these taking an active and leading part in the service. Up to a point this worked, but it was a poor substitute for the much more integrated way of being Church that we had been able to practise in the Riverside School.

By this time the parish was quite widely spread and Hamish Smith, the Congregational member of the Team Ministry, persuaded us of the need to open up a Sunday School of some kind in the far east of Craigshill, in the Letham Primary School.

And so a Sunday Morning Club was started. To run it we persuaded Elizabeth Maitland and several young mothers of the district to 'volunteer'. It proved to have much more appeal than I, for one, had ever expected. Learning through informal club activities seemed to be something that both children and parents enjoyed and benefited from. On the last Sunday of the month, children and parents of the Club came and took part in the St Columba's Family Service. The children didn't just attend. They made their own positive contribution through singing and acting out some of the Bible stories such as the 'Wise and Foolish Builders' and 'Blind Bartimaeus'.

All that we would want to claim for our work with the children in the early years of Livingston New Town is that we struggled all the time to keep it parish-centred, open to all the children of the community, and rejecting everything that would give the impression of being content with a tiny holy huddle for 'those and such as those'. The other big emphasis was on the children themselves being allowed, being encouraged, to take an active part in the Church's life and teaching.

From the insistence of the children being at the heart of the congregation's life, we benefited in all kinds of ways, perhaps mainly through the freshness and vitality of their presence amongst us, but also through the sheer simplicity and practicality of their own belief.

One example here must suffice.

At a Family Service at St Columba's, the minister, just before the prayer of intercession, was asking the congregation for names of any particular causes or persons we should be remembering. There was a fairly lengthy silence and then a little girl's voice rang out from the back of the church: 'Please pray for my Uncle Archie. He goes into hospital tomorrow.'

What was remarkable about this was not just the ring of genuine concern in the child's voice, but, as we discovered next day, taking Uncle Archie into hospital was the beginning of his learning that he was in the early stages of multiple sclerosis. How dreadful it would have been if Archie and his wife had been left to face the ordeal without the prayers, support and encouragement of the Lord's people. But for one child's simplicity of faith, this could well have happened.

One very helpful thing we did with our older children and teenagers was to take them to visit places of historical interest such as the pre-reformation Kirk of Calder in Mid Calder, the Torphichen Preceptory, Linlithgow's ruined palace and its splendid St Michael's Parish Church.

At the Kirk of Calder we used to say something like this:

You will not appreciate this, nor will your children, but your children's children undoubtedly will. The most significant happening this ancient building has witnessed was not in the dim and distant past, but in this very century on 6th January 1966. It was then that the Livingston Ecumenical Experiment was launched at a Service in which, for the first

The Revd Dr James Maitland

St Columba's Church Council with the Revd Norman McCallum and the Revd Dr James Maitland. (Mr A Pirie extreme left; Bert Wardlow extreme right.)   © *The Scotsman*

A meeting of the team ministry: Revd Brian Hardy, Revd Ross McLaren, Revd Dr Jim Maitland, Revd Norman McCallum, Revd Kenneth Hughes and Revd Ken Thornton.

The opening of Lanthorn: Revd Norman McCallum, Revd John Macleod, Revd John Wraight, Revd Joan Ryeland, Revd Dr Jim Maitland and the Revd Ross McLaren.

Revd Norman McCallum (Episcopal priest) and the Revd John Macleod (Church of Scotland minister) administer communion to people in St Columba's Church.

St Columba's celebrates its tenth aniversary. © *Livingston Post/Bob Wallace*

The celebration of the tenth aniversary of the town of Livingston: (left to right) Revd Brian Hardy, Revd Dr Jim Maitland, Revd Hamish Smith, Revd Father John Byrne, Revd Tom Stuckey and Max Cruikshank. © *Livingston Post/Bob Wallace*

The Induction of the Revd Jim Maitland and the Revd Brian Hardy at Midcalder on 6th January 1966.

Eighteen children baptised at St Columba's Church in 1973, by Revd Norman McCallum and Revd Dr Jim Maitland.

© *Church Extension Chimes*

© Life & Work

Mr Alexander Pirie
St Columba's Church

© Life & Work

Dr Margaret Riddoch
St Columba's Church

Miss Betty Robertson
St Columba's Church

The Maitlands move to Knightsridge in 1979: (left to right) Rev Norman McCallum,
Mr Alexander Pirie, Mrs Elizabeth Maitland,
Revd Dr Jim Maitland and Revd Maudeen MacDougall.

Revd Dr Maitland preaching at the Induction of Revd Father John Robinson to St Peter's, Livingston: (left to right) Father John Creanor, Dr Maitland, Bishop Kevin Rafferty and Father John Robinson.

HRH Princess Anne opening an extension to the Family Centre in Knightsridge, which became the new Moss-wood Centre.   © Antonia Reeve Photography

Fiona and Michael Ford
on their wedding day.

Malcolm Drummond, Helen Drummond
and Revd Father John Byrne.

Mr Max Cruikshank, Mrs Maimie Aldous (Team Secretary),
Mrs Pat Cruikshank and Mr Ron Aldous (LDC).

Bhailal and Sharda Patel, early residents of Livingston.

time in Scottish history, Bishop and Presbytery functioned together by inducting the first minister (Church of Scotland) and first priest (Scottish Episcopal Church) to the first ecumenical parish in the country.

At Torphichen Preceptory we learned about the Knights of St John of Malta and about their works of compassion and healing carried through with such caring and commitment. We saw the sanctuary stone in the graveyard that stands to this day as a testimony to the supremacy of right over might and of every person's claim to justice and a fair trial by 'due legal process'. What appealed to us most however was the ancient tombstone that had all the conventional symbols of death—skull and crossbones and hourglass on one side; but on the other, two people getting ready to dance the Highland fling. How readily the children and young people see and appreciate the meaning of this message, and how completely they are switched off by the heavy solemnity and dreariness of what they think is typical church life.

Dance then wherever you may be
I am the Lord of the Dance, said he,
And I'll lead you all wherever you may be
And I'll lead you all in the dance, said he.

~ No 47 (chorus), *Songs of God's People*
(Oxford University Press) ~

The Gospel draws us all, young and old, away from the dance of death and on into the dance of life, into a dancing that involves us with all sorts and conditions of people and with the Lord himself.

While we were still worshipping in the Riverside Primary School, Ron Aldous, the Development Corporation's Social Relations Officer and I, took the older members of Bible Class on a Sunday outing to Whithorn in the South West of Scotland. In the fifth century, St Ninian had his 'head-quarters' here. Here he built his famous *Candida Casa* – White House – Scotland's first building in stone. And from here, Ninian and his followers set about converting the Picts in Scotland to Christianity.

As we started our 'dinner piece', sitting around on or near the site of our earliest Christian settlement, we talked for a time about

Ninian, about how he had been trained in Rome for the Christian priesthood and how he had been sent to be bishop to the Picts. On his journey from Rome to Scotland he visited Martin of Tours in France and seems to have spent several weeks sharing in this man's spirituality and absorbing as much as he could of fresh ways of sharing the Gospel of God's invading Kingdom. What Ninian gained from Martin in Tours became the very stuff of Celtic mission in and far furth of Scotland.

One of the most ancient and best preserved stone carvings in Britain is to be seen in the great cross outside the west door of Iona Abbey. That cross is dedicated to St Martin in gratitude for all he did through Ninian and Columba and so many others to make known the Gospel word, worship and fellowship throughout these islands and in great parts of the continent.

Ninian's mission, like Columba's, seems to have had this out-standing feature. A settlement was always made for the area and all its people, and it consisted not just of a place of worship but a place of everyday work and learning and sharing. The spearhead of their missionary outreach was a team of three. There was someone who could teach better ways of treating the soil and fishing the sea; someone else who had such a feeling for people, their inner conflicts, fears and anxieties that he could be soul-friend, a sensitive and listening counsellor to those with that kind of personal need; and another person who could tell the story of Jesus with something of the freshness and simplicity of the Gospel itself.

How greatly Church life in Scotland would benefit from the Celtic Church's practice of committing itself to an area and all its people. The work of God would then be seen not just in a separate sacred place on a Sunday, but in everything that affects work life, personal and community relationships. These would all be given vibrancy and hope by helping one another across the religious, social and ethnic separations of our time to recognise and draw on the healing, new-creating powers of 'the Kingdom that surely comes'.

I like to think that the Livingston way of trying to be the Lord's mission and ministry of love had enough practical reality in it to let our young folk begin to feel that they themselves had as vital and demanding a part to play as ever Ninian, Columba, Kentigern had in their day.

Growing up in Livingston

In 1970 I was invited to become the chairperson of the newly formed Advisory Committee for Children's Panels in the Lothian Region. The main job of the Committee was to recruit, select and arrange training for people willing to serve at Children's Hearings. This was a radically new way of trying to deal with children up to the age of 16 who had been in trouble with the authorities, usually the police. The child with his/her parent(s) was met, listened to, and talked with by, say, three/four members of the Children's Panel plus the one 'professional', the officially appointed Reporter to the Children's Panel. The essence of this way of working lay in its informality and in the ability of the Panel members to relate to the child and his/her parents. Here was a serious attempt to break with the heavy-handed legalism of the courts and the almost inevitable labelling of the youngster as 'criminal'. The humanity in this approach appealed to us all and, while it could not be expected to give sure-fire answers and a hundred per cent success in every case, it did inspire real confidence and a lot of enthusiasm.

The way in which 'ordinary citizens' responded to the challenge of taking on this kind of time-consuming voluntary service was a heartening discovery for me and for many others. The work here brought me into close contact with people who had wide-ranging experience in this field but, more importantly, had a deep personal commitment to working for a society in Scotland where people and particularly children, whether 'able' or 'differently abled', whatever their status – social, ethnic or religious – will feel wanted, appreciated, welcomed and protected.

Three people to whom I am immensely indebted were Max Paterson, Chief Educational Psychologist for List D Schools in Scotland; Jenny Neilson of St Andrews House Social Work Services group; and John Spencer, Professor of Sociology at Edinburgh University. Through them I learned of a large representative group called 'Growing up in Scotland'. Those I have just named agreed to experiment with a highly localised branch, 'Growing up in Livingston'.

One or two from medical and teaching professions, a social worker, a community worker, three or four parents, two from the

Churches, were personally invited. We met roughly once every four or six weeks for about two years, and all of us benefited in all kinds of ways from this honest sharing of experiences, frustrations and tentative conclusions.

From Livingston's point of view, the most important practical development from this group's deliberations was the pioneer Neighbourhood House in Craigshill. It came about in this way.

The topic for discussion one Sunday evening was Livingston's provision for young mums and toddlers, and the feeling was being strongly expressed that we needed places of easy access from the street. Many found centres and church buildings off-putting and uninviting. One of our medical people was Dr Margaret Riddoch. She told us that the new purpose-built Health Centre in Howden was all but ready for use and would soon be opening. This meant that the house in Ladywell that had served as Health Centre for some seven years would be vacated at an early date. 'Why not,' said Margaret Riddoch, 'press the Development Corporation to have it continue as a drop-in centre for mothers and toddlers?' We did this right away only to receive the dustiest of dusty answers from the Board: 'We are charged with building dwelling houses for the people and factories for industry. To give up even one such dwelling house for a recreation centre would be completely out of order.'

It took something like five years and umpteen meetings and a change of Board Chairman to bring about a change of policy. But changed it was and Livingston Development Corporation made available a house at 31 Canberra Street in 1974. This became the greatly appreciated Neighbourhood House that not only did magnificent work for the people around, especially the mothers and toddlers, but provided an inspiring model for other areas in the town where each was provided with its own 'Neighbourhood House'. Such places in the early years of any district are so essential for countering loneliness and for strengthening the rudiments of a caring community life.

In Craigshill we were particularly fortunate in the two people who volunteered to run the place – Chris McGavin and Eleanor Douglas. After some months Eleanor had to withdraw, but Chris proved herself capable not just of coping, but of giving the house an openness, a friendliness and a sense of purpose that did more than anything else for the stability and liveliness of life amongst the families in the surrounding streets.

Another thing that worked strongly in our favour here was the willingness of the Young Women's and Young Men's to support the venture in every way they could. The Young Women's Christian Association was formed just over one hundred years ago 'as a trans-denominational body to build a worldwide fellowship through which women and girls may come to know more of the love of God as revealed in Jesus Christ for themselves and for all people and may learn to express that love in responsible action'. How quietly, how effectively, Chris McGavin, her helpers and backers, fulfilled the vision of the first founders and did so in this little bit of God's world without any fanfare of trumpets or big-time pub-licity. Here again was the salt of the earth still working silently giving taste to life and countering the influences making for decay and corruption.

CHAPTER 7

Working the Parish: Craigshill

THE Scottish Episcopal Church in 1971 sent us a second member of the Team Ministry, Norman McCallum. He had completed his ministerial training at Coates Hall in Edinburgh and joined the Team after doing a year's work as a social worker in Livingston, a quite excellent preparation for the job we would be expecting him to do.

At that time the pattern of ministry in the Ecumenical Parish was as follows. The Church of Scotland minister would serve as parish minister in Craigshill, where the church building – St Columba's – belonged to the Church of Scotland. In Ladywell/ Howden Brian Hardy, Episcopal priest, would be parish minister with his base at St Paul's, the church building put up by the Scottish Episcopal Church. In Dedridge the Congregational member of the Team Ministry would be parish minister, working in and from the Lanthorn building. In the Lanthorn set-up, the Methodist member of the Team, Joan Ryeland, shared the work from very early on.

Norman McCallum, the Team decided, should work with me in Craigshill. Despite the disparity in age – or perhaps *because* of it – this arrangement worked very well indeed, both in the leading of services at St Columba's and in the working of the parish, Craigshill, the population of which was then around the 8000 mark.

At that time the feeling in the Team was that we should not use the term 'elder' because it was so strongly bound up with one par-ticular denomination in the co-operating churches. So, to do the work that elders are supposed to do in the Church of Scotland, we had *councillors* – ie members of St Columba's Church Council; and *counsellors* – ie people who were tackling the pastoral job with the families in the different streets. A person could be both councillor and counsellor, but only if he or she were prepared to do both jobs with some commitment and enthusiasm.

Unless a street were impossibly large, the usual arrangement was for one person to be counsellor for that street. Working with the counsellor in every street, we had a team of visitors, each visitor responsible for up to twenty homes. It was the visitor's job to deliver the church's quarterly newsletter to every home, to try to build up a good-neighbourly relationship with each family, and to keep the counsellor informed as to any special needs discovered among his or her 'parishioners' – for example, the birth of a new baby, a child starting school, illness, or a family bereavement.

From this way of working it can be seen how determined we all were to keep the parish, with every family in it, with every soul in it, as our chief concern. This was a huge undertaking and one that required constant and supportive attentiveness by the ministers, counsellors and visitors.

For day-to-day working of the parish, Norman had responsibility for Craigshill South and myself for Craigshill North. The pastoral demands of the work became so pressing that we had to meet for one or two hours on Wednesday afternoons to talk through the information, problems, suggestions, that kept pouring in from counsellors and visitors. From all this it was clear that the Gospel was coming alive for some families. There were others, however, where the entire household seemed unaffected, not to say *dis*affected, and alienated. How could we keep touch with them? How could we let 'the Man for others' break through to them? No quick or easy answers were ever forthcoming. However, both Norman and I were convinced that real and loving contacts with the unchurched had to be maintained, if only that we might the better hear what the Lord was saying in and through them and their 'outsiderness'.

For the better sharing of the 'bad and the good', on Wednesday afternoons we had the help of one of our counsellors, Betty Robertson, and later on of another counsellor, Jean Gray, both of whom were already doing a full time job in parish work. Betty was a deeply devout person with a childlike faith in the power of prayer. Jean had worked for some years with the Church in New Zealand and had a great deal to teach us on the counselling side of the work here. This regular, frank and prayerful sharing of experiences and ideas did a great deal to keep us on our feet spiritually and to keep us looking for that renewal of community life and church life promised to us in the Kingdom of God.

In 1977 the Team decided that Norman should be given full ministerial responsibility for Craigshill and that I should be given the job of starting up the church in Knightsridge, a recently developed area in the north of the town, at that time part of St Paul's parish.

Norman, very soon after my departure, initiated a way of strengthening the hands of the District Counsellors by appointing a co-ordinator for every three districts. This, in my view, was a simple but quite brilliant way of dealing with the new situation, so that now the pastoral load was being shared more fully between counsellors and minister. People with obvious pastoral gifts were being given the chance to make the most of these in the ongoing work of allowing fresh living social tissue to form and grow in the life of the streets.

The ministerial changeover could well have allowed Norman and the counsellors to shelve the community dimension of the work and to concentrate entirely on 'building up the congregation'. As I see it, that would have been a denial of the wholeness of the ecumenical vision given to us at the beginning and how glad I was that Norman would have nothing to do with it.

Shortly after this, Norman's Bishop, Alastair Haggart, decided that the time had come for Norman to move from Livingston. For that decision the Bishop had undoubtedly many sound and compelling reasons, but the ecumenical nature of the work in Livingston didn't seem to be given the priority place it should have had. In a quite tense session with the Bishop, the entire Team pleaded for Norman to be left in Livingston for a few more years yet. I threw in my own tuppence worth, and Norman kept saying, 'I don't feel that the work I was given to do in Livingston is anywhere near completion'. The Bishop was adamant, however, and Norman was moved out.

This happened not because the Bishop was uncaring about his priests, their needs and convictions. Quite the reverse was true. Nor could it ever be said that the Bishop was lacking in ecumenical concern and commitment. No one could have been more supportive and encouraging to the Livingston 'ecumaniacs' than he was. This happened, I believe, because the Bishop had little or no realisation of the community/church dimension that had been in the forefront of the work in Craigshill for the past ten years, a dimension that Norman was uniquely equipped to recognise and to serve.

The failure to communicate this to the Bishop and to others was ours in the Team.

The inward-lookingness, the defensiveness as well as the deep dividedness of the Church in Scotland's parishes have been infinitely damaging not only to church life, but still more to community life. Few in the Churches' leadership, however, pay serious attention, and fewer still point the way to repentance and a simpler obedience. A word from the Council of Churches in the Philippines has to be taken into soul and conscience by everyone who has a care for the regeneration of Christian life in Scotland.

> *A new political incarnation is already being brought to the birth. This requires a renewed Church that will be a companion in the making of a new society ... living a spirituality of justice and freedom and rooted among the poor.*

I believe that nothing less than a 'new political incarnation' becomes an inescapable consequence of thoroughgoing ecumenical commitment on the part of the Churches' people, ministerial and lay. What we found in Craigshill, and again in Knightsridge, was that a strong sense of companionship between the ecumenical congregation and the local community did strongly develop for the enrichment and strengthening of both.

One vital point of contact between church and parish was the school, both primary and secondary. Craigshill High made its own contribution, mainly through the members of staff who were committed and active members of the Church, but also through teachers who would never have professed allegiance to any Church but who had a profound care for the children and their growth in awareness of the values that give life its only ultimate worth and meaning.

All of us in the Team Ministry had reason for ever-deepening thankfulness to the Head Teacher in Craigshill High, Alexander Pirie, and his colleagues, not only for the way they made the different ministers feel welcome and at home in the school, but still more for the unending patience with which they struggled to retain a spiritual dimension in the school's morning assembly. I used to think that the resentment of anything and everything smacking of conventional religion was at least as much due to some members of staff as to the students. It was so good for us ministers to see and feel for ourselves the yawning chasm between ourselves and these youngsters of our time and town.

Sandy Pirie had come to Livingston from the north of Scotland and had been warned by some of his church friends there against having any truck with these way-out ecumaniacs he'd find in his new quarters. In the event Sandy discovered that the ecumenical congregation, its ministers and ways of worshipping and working, were so lively and appealing that without hesitation he threw in his lot with us. And so did Rena Pirie, his wife. Together they made a deeply valued contribution to the development of church life in Livingston.

Sandy soon became a Presbytery elder and it was here, I believe, he did most for us in the Ecumenical Parish. To have him on the Business Committee was not just to 'have a friend at court', but to have among the often doubting and questioning Presbyterian brethren a strong ambassador for the ecumenical way of working. Scotland is going to need many Sandy Piries if our places of worship are indeed to become 'both a sanctuary and a light'.

Four Men of Craigshill

Bert Wardlaw

Bert had spent the greater part of his working life as a long distance truck driver. He was as familiar with the roads of Britain and the places they led to, as the rest of us were with the different streets and ways in and about Livingston. He also knew the stress such a job can cause and for the last year or so his health suffered quite considerably.

He had been taken into hospital with serious chest trouble and at one point his life was in the balance. He did recover not just something of his good health, but also a new kind of religious faith

– out of the blue it seemed. In the midst of his illness he had been brought face to face with the Lord in a way that was utterly convincing and life-changing.

Before he left the ward he insisted on telling something of this experience to his Consultant and asked him to let the minister at St Columba's know about him. In this way I came to meet the only person of my acquaintance who became a believer through a Damascus road experience. 'Whether in the body or out of the body,' he would say, 'I cannot tell, but this encounter had something so wonderful in it that such time as is left to me must be spent for Him.'

Bert spent literally hours every day reading his Bible – Old Testament and New Testament. He never missed a church service on Sunday. He loved flowers and all green and growing things, and not only kept a good garden at home but insisted on looking after the manse garden as well. He would never accept a penny in payment. He enjoyed painting and seemed to find a way of expressing his feelings, his deep thankfulness, in art that he found nowhere else. His conversation was that of a man who much preferred to listen than to talk. Again and again he quite unconsciously left one with the strong conviction that there goes a man whose one over-riding concern is: 'That I be ready when he comes for me.' In this at least he eminently succeeded, for right to the end the Bible was giving him the light he needed, and waiting on the Lord the quiet confidence he radiated so clearly.

The story of Bert Wardlaw's last years used to put me in mind of that spiritual giant of this century, Simone Weil of France (1909-45). She tells how she discovered George Herbert's poem 'Love'. She learned it by heart and used to recite it to herself again and again, 'concentrating all my attention upon it and clinging with all my soul to the tenderness it enshrines .... It was during one of these recitations that Christ himself came down and took possession of me. Until last September I had never prayed in all my life'.

Love bade me welcome; yet my soul drew back
Guilty of dust and sin
But quick-eyed Love observing me grow slack
From my first entrance in

Drew near to me, sweetly questioning
 If I lacked anything

'A guest,' I answered 'worthy to be here'
 Love said, 'you shall be he'
'I the unkind, ungrateful? Ah my dear,
 I cannot look on thee'
Love took my hand and smiling did reply
 'Who made the eyes but I?'

'Truth, Lord, but I have marred them; let my shame
 Go where it doth deserve'
'And know you not,' says Love, 'who bore the blame?'
 'My dear then I will serve'
'You must sit down,' says Love, 'and taste my meat'
 So I did sit and eat.
       ~ *George Herbert (1593-1633)* ~

John Ross

John and Nan Ross came to Livingston in 1970 when John came to
take up the Headship of Riverside Primary School in Craigshill.
Right from the start he revelled in the work there and took a
special delight in getting to know the children, the poorest among
them being of particular personal concern to him. He was a big
man, but his size, far from over-awing the children, seemed to make
them feel the reality of his and the school's protecting care.

He was not a church man in the conventional sense, but he
cared passionately for what the Gospel calls 'God's Kingdom and
his justice', and he cared equally for peace. It was this caring that
made him work so hard for Livingston as the first chairperson of
the town's pioneer Community Council. In the re-organisation of
local government, this kind of town-wide council was shelved in
favour of Community Councils for the different districts – much, I
believe, to the detriment of our corporate sense of identity as a
town.

It was this same concern for justice and peace that made him
take on the agent's job for Ross McLaren, member of the Team

Ministry, when he stood as Liberal Democratic candidate for Livingston South in the Lothian Regional Council election of 1982. To do a job like this, John needed to believe not only in the policies of the political party, but also in the candidate as a person of commitment and integrity. Because these two came together in Ross McLaren, John was able as agent to head up a lively and successful campaign in the 1982 election.

Enthusiast as he was in local politics, as in everything else, he nevertheless had a detachment from party and allegiance to party that to my mind is the mark of maturity in democratic practice and understanding. I remember congratulating him on giving up the best part of a week's holiday to go door-knocking for the Liberal Democrats in a bye-election in England. John's response was characteristically different: 'Yes, we won.' Then, after a pause and with deep feeling, he said: 'Jim, never give your heart to any political party.' This outlook will not lead to political stardom, but it does leave room for people, and the making of relationships between people, as the very stuff of daily living.

Two things especially John helped me to learn about working with children. One was the vital importance of the children's active participation in the business of learning and sharing. Every week a class would take the lead in portraying some Bible story in a simple dramatic presentation. Sometimes they would display their paintings of the different scene(s), and always they would tell the story in their own words as if it happened only yesterday in the streets of Livingston. Often I came away from these assemblies feeling that we had all been drawn into an actual happening.

The second thing has to do with commending the way of love to the children. If we are to do this in ways that let our words ring true, then we ourselves have to be loving people – parents, teachers and ministers. 'Children,' he used to say, 'have a devastating power of seeing us for what we truly are.'

Two illustrations of John's own rootedness in love are worth relating.

When our daughter Barbara was married, the St Columba's building had not been long in use and arrangements for cleaning, dusting, and so on, were not properly in place. John and Nan Ross discovered just a couple of days before the wedding that the church 'could do with a proper wash'. Without any fuss or talk, John and Nan spent the night before the wedding scrubbing, cleaning and polishing that great expanse of floor. A school 'heidie' he might be, a recognised community leader he certainly was, but John's view of loving the neighbour left no way of avoiding the most menial tasks.

Though the congregation was now worshipping at St Columba's, we were still dependent on the Riverside Primary School for the main part of our Sunday School work. This meant using not only several different classrooms for actual teaching, but also taking space to store equipment from Sunday to Sunday, and also finding ways of keeping intact the children's project work often stretching over several weeks. No one could have been more co-operative and helpful than John Ross was. He must have had to listen to a lot of moaning and complaining from janitor, cleaners, and even teachers, but he never made us feel that we were a nuisance and should be looking for accommodation elsewhere. How well the ancient tag fitted this man: 'Where there's heart-room, there's house-room.'

The best example of John's belief in openness to others – especially to the others who are different – was seen in his attitude to the Catholic Church. Remember, he was not a church man, and sometimes he was not above making a little song and dance about his own agnosticism. However, Religious Education was part of the syllabus and was not to be by-passed or scamped whatever the pressures from our secularist/consumerist society. Mrs Dorothy Brown, Assistant Head at the school and herself a Methodist Lay Preacher, did an outstanding job in this area and helped some of her colleagues to do the same. John Ross's biggest contribution here came through his invitation to Father John Byrne to meet the children in Primaries VI and VII. This question and answer session was as big a success with the teachers as with the children and opened the way for the Church of Scotland minister to be invited to a similar session in St Andrew's Primary. In addition, Sister Pauline from St Andrew's Church was invited to take part in school assemblies and to meet with groups from the Riverside top classes.

This simple 'come and go' at school level is of immense importance in allowing the ecumenical outlook to take on new meaning and reality among children – and also among at least some of the parents and teachers.

These are just a few of the reasons why the name and memory of John Ross should be honoured in Livingston. Those who knew him best would want to say that it was not so much what he did, as what he was as a person that really mattered. His brightness and sparkle, his sense of humour and sense of fun, the genuineness of his love for children and his God-given ability to meet and mix and be at home with all sorts and conditions of people – such qualities made him an inspiration in the community.

Frank Heyes

Frank Heyes was the second medical doctor to be appointed to Livingston. He and Mary, his wife, from the new town of Harlow in England, came here partly because of the Livingston Medical Experiment and partly because of the Ecumenical Experiment. They were both strongly active members of the Anglican/Episcopal Church and used to say that it was their experience of new town living in Harlow that made them eager for 'more of the same'. Scotland allowed the Livingston Medical Experiment to split their time between general practice and developing a specialist interest in the local hospital. The set-up appeals to those who are keen to do the work of a local general practitioner, but are also just as keen to keep abreast of the ongoing work in the specialist field of particular interest to them. My own view is that this way of working has served Livingston well and has given us doctors who not only keep up with developments in one particular area of medical research and practice, but seem motivated by this very experience to keep themselves abreast of ongoing developments in general practice throughout the country.

After some years in the Craigshill team, Frank came to feel that he would like to have Industrial Medicine as his specialist concern. This was not provided for in the Livingston Medical Experiment and after, I am sure, careful consideration by the medical people responsible, Frank Heyes' suggested scheme was turned down. Frank and many others in Livingston were bitterly disappointed and before long Frank moved to take up an appointment with British Rail in Glasgow, a move that was a big loss for Livingston but undoubted gain for Scottish Industrial Medicine.

Three things stand out for me about Frank Heyes.

First was his belief in the need for younger people, not just in Livingston but throughout the country, to allow themselves to be 'freed up' from 'old wives' tales' about health and healthy living. He used to say that one of the blessings about a new town was that granny had been left behind! Coming from a person as gentle and loving as Frank, this shocked many of us; but it made us 'think again' about the past and its constraining effect on the kind of life we want for ourselves and our children.

Second, Frank was the first authoritative voice I heard raised against 'the pollution of noise'. It may be that in the end of the day we shall discover that more lasting damage is done to us all by the constant roar of our cities' traffic, than from the fumes pouring from exhausts. There are doctors who claim that actual physical damage is done to the hearing of young people attending discos. If this is true for our physical make-up, how much more hurtful it must be to our psyches. Perhaps there is a closer connection than we like to think between excessively noisy surroundings and attempted escape into the world of violence, self-indulgence and drug abuse.

The third big contribution Frank made to life in Livingston came through the leading part he took in Forum and its concerns. After the churches went their separate ways to their separate buildings, Frank manfully took on the chairing of the rump Forum and succeeded in having questions affecting the town and its shaping responsibly discussed. Numbers were small, but the few went on meeting Sunday after Sunday in Craigs Farm Centre. One of the few was John Hoey. John became Warden of the Farm and in that position gained for himself, and for Craigs Farm, a reputation for community concern and openness to people that has gone far beyond Livingston.

I sat beside John at Frank's funeral in St Cuthbert's Church, Colinton. While we were waiting for the service to start, John spoke about all he owed to Frank and of the powerful influence he had had on him and others through his chairing of the struggling little Forum. 'He was so human,' said John, 'so ready to see the humour in things. Never took himself and his views too seriously, but was always looking for ways of letting the little people, the forgotten people, begin to come into their own.'

From John Hoey that was praise indeed, and praise that should help make everyone in present day Livingston realise how real is the debt we owe to the Frank Heyes of this world.

Tom Welsh

My first contact with Tom Welsh was on the telephone one bleak morning in October. He said simply: 'I have just been sent home from the Western General Hospital in Edinburgh. The Consultant there says I've got cancer and I'll be lucky to live till Christmas. I don't know what to do or where to turn.'

I called later in the day and found him a typical well-to-do working man in mid-life, thrown down to the depths by the word that his days were numbered. We talked – he, his wife Mary, and myself – and as we tried to share the heartbreak, longing and confusion, a quiet of mind began to take hold of us and we were able not just to talk, but to pray.

I cannot remember what words came out. I'm sure they must have been hesitant and fumbling – but a sense of the Presence was given to us, an encounter with the Living One not dissimilar to Mary of Magdala's meeting with the Lord in the garden on the first Easter morning. Face to face with death, we felt somehow freed from its threatening terror. Whatever the future held of pain, weakness, soul-quenching separation, a strange assurance of life in ever greater fullness was given to the three of us. This awareness was particularly strong for Tom and never really left him.

He had to spend the greater part of every day in bed. He was well cared for by the district nurse and a particularly able doctor and, of course, his wife's strong calm and loving devotion was the biggest factor in maintaining the peace and brightness of their home. Every day we had prayer together.

Tom lived beyond Christmas and right through to Easter. In November he had made Mary buy daffodil bulbs and two or three rose bushes. 'They'll be flowering,' he said, 'after I'm gone.' And they were. On the day of the funeral the daffodils were beginning to blossom out in the golden cleanness of a new Spring.

At the crematorium we sang George Matheson's hymn:

I lay in dust life's glory dead
*   And from the ground*
There blossoms red
Life that shall endless be.

~ Hymn 677, *Church Hymnary* (Third Edition) ~

Some three years later Mary Welsh was with us all for our week on Iona. During one of the sessions, Mary spoke to the group of Tom, her late husband, and how down and despairing she had been when the news of his cancer and impending death was broken to her. 'The strange thing,' she went on to say, 'was that in the event, these months from October through to Easter and after, were the happiest days of our married life.'

So Mary of Magdala went and told the disciples that she had seen the Lord and related to them all that he had told her.

~ John 20: 18 ~

CHAPTER 8

Working the Parish: Knightsridge

KNIGHTSRIDGE is an area in the north of Livingston that has some 6000 people. From early on, and for various reasons, it came to be regarded as the Cinderella of the new town. It was in the St Paul's parish, but no more than half a dozen families made any real link with their parish church – in the completely separate district of Ladywell, on the other side of the busy district road.

The only public buildings were the Knightsridge Primary School and, years later, St Kenneth's Roman Catholic Primary School. In addition there was a Sports Pavilion built to serve the needs of youngsters using the nearby football pitch.

In 1979 the Team decided I should be moved from Craigshill to Knightsridge and given the remit of trying to develop some kind of indigenous church there. The challenge appealed to both Elizabeth and myself and soon we were able to leave the manse in Craigshill to make our home at 70 Cameron Way, a corporation house cheek-by-jowl with the Harvester Pub.

John Wraight, successor to Brian Hardy, shared ministry at St Paul's with Maudeen McDougall, Church of Scotland, and they both had agreed with the Team's view that Knightsridge should be worked as a parish by itself with its own centre of worship. John introduced us to the group of Knightsridge people whom he re-garded as the nucleus for the new congregation and without delay we began to meet for worship and quite informal discussion on Sunday mornings in the Sports Pavilion at the end of Ferguson Way.

Already there was a strong Catholic congregation worshipping in Knightsridge Primary at noon on Sundays. The young priest, Mike Freyne, was based further west in Carmondean, but he worked this part of his parish with great cheerfulness and dedication and was good to work with, especially in common concerns for com-munity issues.

One of the first jobs we were invited to do together was to arrange and officiate at a special service to mark the inauguration of Knightsridge Community Council. This was well attended by the new members of the Council and by people from the different 'Ways'. Both Mike and I were grateful for the means by which a launching of this kind could help make clear to all and sundry that in Knightsridge at least the people and ministry of both churches had a priority concern for the life and well-being of their own community and for everything affecting its outlook and future.

The Sports Pavilion soon became too small for our Sunday morning congregation, so we decided to move to Knightsridge Primary School hall. We met at ten, so we were 'skailing', leaving, while the Catholics were arriving. This 'rubbing shoulders', and thereby passing the time of day, chatting back and forth, did far more than anyone would imagine to overcome the traditional strangeness between Catholic and Protestant and to make for easy, kindly relations between us. This good-neighbourly relationship found expression in a Christmas play performed by the children of the two congregations. Sharing a building, even the local school hall, can do so much to let the Spirit rescue us from our alien and alienating ways.

At the beginning we found ourselves much poorer off for musical accompaniment and strong lead singers than the Catholic congregation was. How ready they were to help us out! Indeed a young mother whose playing of the guitar was highly professional and whose singing voice was a joy for us all, took part in the early part of our service and then helped the children with their singing – and their Sunday School lessons! After all that, she joined her own people for their mass at noon.

Our strategy for developing church life in Knightsridge had five strands to it.

The first ran from the Morning Service out into the homes and concerns of the people making up the community.

At every Morning Service a very important and sizable place was given to what is usually called the 'Intimations Slot', but which we called 'News Time'. Here people were encouraged to take time to tell us about the people in their Way, or their own part of the Way. For example:

- 'A new baby has arrived three doors down from us';
- 'A family has just moved into No 23';
- 'Mrs Smith at 74 has been ill and is now in hospital' or 'Mr Jones has just come home from hospital';
- 'People in our street are very keen to run a babysitting scheme. Any willing to help please talk with me at the end of the service';
- 'Seats have been booked for Pantomime in Edinburgh four weeks on Monday. Names and money to be handed in at end of the Service';
- 'Old Mrs Elliott is celebrating her 75th birthday on Wednesday. A birthday card is on the table in the vestibule. Please don't forget to sign';
- 'Many more volunteers are needed for the Disabled Persons Club. Names to me please at the close of the Service' …

… and so on. Jim Nicol, one of our Church Counsellors, was an active member of the Community Council from its inception and served for many years as its tireless chairperson. Every other Sunday, sometimes more often, he would tell us about the Council and some of the problems it was working on. Most days there was a 'plug' for the next meeting of the Council and for people to show interest by attending.

All of this served to keep us alive to the realities of life 'out there', but also helped to keep earthed our prayers of intercession for the parish and all its people.

Our prayer for others was seen as so important that we had to tackle it in two sections: one concerned with the world of nations, especially the so-called Third World; the other with our own community, local and nationwide.

The World Council of Churches' Ecumenical Prayer Cycle – 'With All God's People' – proved quite invaluable by deepening our awareness of global realities and by widening and enriching our prayer experience through drawing us into sharing the actual prayers of people whose church life and culture were very different from our own.

We had a group of five people who took it in turns to lead our world intercessions by giving a brief account of the nation or group of nations who were our concern for that week, pointing out their position on the world globe, and then leading us all in prayers for the country or countries, very often in words made and used by the people of these countries themselves. Here are some examples:

> O God, we bring before you the people of Latin America whose suf-fering seems to have no end, tearing our hearts apart and challenging our faith in the God of justice. In spite of the suffering we want to be instruments of reconciliation, not allowing hate to be the motivation behind our struggles to eradicate injustice. Listen to the pleas of your people. Amen.

In Ecuador repayments on international loans cost millions of dollars a year, while every half hour a child dies from malnutrition:

> I hunger and I eat, three times a day – or more;
> They hunger and they do not eat,
> They hunger and they do not eat,
> They hunger and they do not eat;
> Help me to help them.

Mid-Week Prayers

The second strand issued from our prayers on a Wednesday night, prayers that every other week centred on a celebration of Holy Communion. The distinctive feature of this gathering was shared Bible study on the main passage for next Sunday's Morning Ser-vice. Here the minister's comments were kept to a bare minimum, but each member of the group, usually around 15, was expected to give his/her honest opinion of the passage before us and also to listen closely to the views of others. No instant summing-up was ever attempted on the night, but come Sunday morning the minister was expected to weave his sermon from the strands contributed on the Wednesday evening. This was far from simple and I would not claim even fifty per cent success, but again people were gradually coming to feel that the Gospel story was a story for them. Not only was it for them, but it was such that they themselves were caught up in the action. It was the people of Knightsridge at our Wednesday evening gatherings who first helped me to realise that so-called 'narrative theology' has to be the very stuff of Church thinking and Church preaching.

This mid-week service had two notable features. Four of our 'regulars' attended the charismatic gathering at St Andrew's Catholic Church in Craigshill. Very often we would hear from one or other of the four about new songs to new tunes. Sometimes one would tell of a 'word' given by a person reading haltingly from the Bible and then saying how its truth came home to him or her, thus managing to convey new confidence and strength in a quite unexpected way.

One person who joined us on most Wednesday evenings was a lapsed Catholic, an alcoholic with a very keen intelligence. She would make voluble contributions, but she never talked nonsense and sometimes it seemed that the mind of the Lord was finding expression through her in a particularly clear and sometimes quite disturbing way.

Later on, Flo was found to be terminally ill with cancer of the liver. The Care Group convenor for her Way was able to tell Flo's story to her parish priest. He immediately visited her, took time and no little trouble to restore her to full communion and had her sharing the mass day after day. Her Care Group visitor spoke often of the transformation that took place in Flo, her appearance, surroundings and the atmosphere of her home, so that her death when it came had in it something of a strange and wonderful beauty.

At mid-week prayers, as in so much of church life in Knightsridge, two people – Stuart Dickson and his wife Rose – by their enthusiasm and the depth and simplicity of their own faith and, most of all, by their all-embracing practice of prayer, did more than they will ever know to allow the Gospel to have a freer course amongst us all.

Church Meeting

Another very important, though never very popular, strand in our parish strategy lay in the Church Meeting, which in Knightsridge was held quarterly as part of Sunday morning worship. It was the Congregationalists among us who taught us the importance of this practice, so central to their tradition. Despite some resistance and a few mutterings, we persevered with the Church Meeting, partly out of loyalty to our ecumenical partners, but also because some of us at least were convinced that if we were aiming to be a church of the people, then the people must be given proper opportunity to voice their questions, criticisms, suggestions on everything concerning the church's life and mission.

As might be expected, finance had a place at every Church Meeting, but was never allowed to dominate. Some of the issues we tried to work through were these:

- Ways for the church to support Community Council;
- Appeals both through the Community Council and direct to the Development Corporation and the West Lothian District Council for better provision in the way of a proper Community Centre for Knightsridge;
- How to recruit leaders for youth work and teachers for Sunday School;
- What to do about the jam-packed houses in Knightsridge IV district;
- How to shape up better to our Third World responsibilities.

One of our liveliest Church Meeting discussions was on the question of the frequency of Communion celebrations. Because of the tightness of our Sunday morning schedule at the school, we could not make the same provision for the Episcopal people in Knightsridge as that at St Columba's, St Paul's and Lanthorn, so the proposal was made to have one other Sunday morning celebration, in addition to the regular celebration on the first Sunday of the month. And then for the other two weeks in the month there would be a celebration at Mid-Week Prayers at 70 Cameron Way.

Two men who had been elders long before coming to Livingston spoke strongly against the proposal. Their main reason for objecting was that, in their view, a more frequent observance would 'take away from the awesomeness of the sacramental experience'. One of our congregation's most active members was Kathleen Gosden, a deeply devout Episcopal Church person. In course of discussion she said: 'I was confirmed when I was seven and I have shared communion every Sunday since. Far from this frequency making the Sacrament commonplace and everyday, it has become increasingly meaningful and precious for me.' This simple statement from personal experience was unanswerable and carried the day.

And so we were moved one tiny step nearer the point when the Lord's Supper, Holy Communion, the Eucharist, will come to be seen as central to every main act of Christian worship.

Care Groups

The fourth strand in our mission strategy centred on our Care Groups out in the streets.

Here we searched for a committed Church person, Protestant or Catholic, willing to take a kindly and responsible interest in twenty families in his/her immediate vicinity. This interest would be expected to find expression along lines like these:

1 Trying to get to know the different families and patiently working away to build up friendly and real relationships with them.
2 Delivering the church newsletter at Christmas, Easter and early Autumn. In making this delivery, stress was laid on the importance of the Care Group member making personal contact with an adult in each home and not just pushing the news sheet through the letter box. So many publications are delivered to every home in any one week that many people will do little more than give a casual glimpse in their direction, if that. Better to call back again, and yet again, until someone in the house has been seen and spoken with.
3 Taking a special interest in the children – birthdays, schooling, the youth organisation to which they may or could belong, making a note of their first name and greeting them on the street, at the shops, at church on Sunday.
4 *Most important of all:* each family in the group of twenty is to be prayed for by name at least once per week, and every day when there is trouble in the house.

With this last requirement we found some Church of Scotland

people hesitant and inclined to shrug it off as 'way out of the box'. Catholics and Baptists, on the other hand, seemed to see the importance of this part of the commitment very readily and were willing to take it on, and by their eagerness commended the practice to the doubters.

We liked to have a committed Church person in every street as a kind of mother/father figure for the other Care Group members, so that there was always someone to whom they could turn for guidance and support.

We tried hard to establish the pattern of all the Care Group members meeting for an hour every three months; the minister and, wherever possible, the parish priest, attending as well. These little meetings could sometimes be frustrating, sometimes humbling, and sometimes quite uplifting, as when the young priest, Brian Saddler, was around to lead the singing – but always they were informative and spiritually strengthening.

Giving Children their Place

The fifth strand was our work with the children and young people. Our main allies in this area of parish life were the teachers in the Knightsridge Primary School. Head Teacher, Harry Cockburn, and his assistant Heads, first Mrs Eleanor Shaw then Mrs Kathleen Moir, were caring, co-operative people who had the kind of feeling for children that gave their word that directness and simplicity characteristic of all inspired teaching. It certainly helped greatly to make Wednesday's Morning Assemblies spiritually profitable occasions for us all. The Infant Mistress at that time, Miss Jan Hutchison, was a deeply committed Christian herself and gave a big place in her Religious Education teaching to singing evangelical choruses with appropriate 'actions'.

I saw then that one of our main responsibilities as the parish church was to support, encourage and affirm these teachers and their colleagues as they met and dealt with all the non-Catholic children of our community.

My own direct contribution to the life of the school was minimal. The first part of every Wednesday morning was spent at the school, just being there and sharing, mostly as one of the congregation, the weekly worship service. How impressive and challenging it was to see the care and thoughtfulness that went into the choice of the different singings and the teaching of tunes and words, the sincerity and brevity of the prayers, often led by the children themselves, and the 'children's address' so freshly prepared and professionally delivered. I used to leave the school thinking how privileged I was as parish minister to have a school like this and teachers like these at the very heart of the parish life. Our prayers for the children, their parents and their teachers on a Sunday and during the week had a ring of greater expectancy in them because of the minister's Wednesday morning at school.

My one grouse against the Head here was that he, in my view, concentrated too exclusively on the school's own quality of life and education. This meant that the community, in which the school had to do its vitally important job, was never regarded as a powerful entity in itself, the thinness and harshness of whose life could be so strongly militating against the work the teachers were so valiantly tackling day by day. Take one example. The school, like every other public building in the area, suffered terribly from attacks of vandalism, but so far as I know this was seen as something to be tholed as best we could, while the question of the underlying causes was left to others. It seemed to me that an initiative might well have been taken by the school and its staff to expose and highlight the reasons for the anti-social behaviour on the part of a tiny minority. To involve teachers, parents and perhaps some of the older children with the Regional Councillors, District Councillors, Community Education workers, and people from the Development Corporation, as well as the police, could have done much to heighten awareness within the school and throughout the area of where exactly 'the shoe was pinching' for families and their children.

However regrettable – for people like me – this 'isolationist' policy on the part of the Head Teacher might seem, the school, because of the dedication and genuine concern on the part of the teachers and their Head, was the main life-enhancing influence in the locality, and for this we could never be too thankful.

Youth work in Knightsridge was no easier than anywhere else. The Boys' Brigade struggled to establish a Company, but in the end, after great effort, they had to admit defeat. The Girls' Brigade did well, however – as did the Scouts and Guides. The setting up and maintenance of the Adventure Playground was perhaps the greatest achievement on the youth service side, and here a quite unrepayable debt of gratitude is due to the Save the Children Fund for such generous support in money and personnel.

Our Sunday School work was heavy-going at times because of difficulty in recruiting teachers. Many children came around, partly because of church members like Miriam Scotland, who used to collect five, six, seven children from among the neighbours and bring them to the Service at ten o'clock. Three people at that time made a sterling contribution to the work we were trying to do with the children. These were Margaret and Alan Mercer, who ran the Sunday School for a whole year, and Margaret Hardy, who travelled from Bathgate, five miles, every Sunday morning to take our Senior Section. These and others with them not only did a demanding job in a purposeful and business-like fashion, but they found ways of letting something of the Lord's love for the children come through their words and their work.

We were taught and re-taught two big lessons in Knightsridge. In all our dealings with the children as Christian parents, teachers, counsellors or ministers, we have to set top of our agenda the words of Jesus: 'Suffer the little children to come to me.' He doesn't say, 'Make sure they're properly schooled in the Scriptures or even in my teaching'. He doesn't say keep them coming to a synagogue/church/temple. He *does* say, however, that if we are to play fair by the children, if our words are to convey to them something more than the bare meaning, then, for us who would share the Gospel with the children entrusted to us, God's Christ must be livingly, lovingly present encompassing us all – children, parents, friends, neighbours. For this to happen, for the Gospel to come alive in this way for the children and ourselves, then everything we attempt to do with and for the children must be saturated through and through with prayer and the mind of Christ given in prayer, before, during and after our direct encounter with the Lord in his children on Sunday at church, and every day at home. Saint Augustine used to say to people working with children: 'What you say to John about God does matter, but what you say to God about John matters infinitely more.'

The other big lesson for us in the Knightsridge experience had to do with the children's own active participation in the life and worship and concerns of the Church.

Jesus' words about the children are very unexpected and shocking for us adult men and women who fondly imagine that we have to do all the teaching and the children have to do all the learning. Jesus, however, says something quite different. If you want to know what the Kingdom of Heaven is like, look closely at the children. They share the life of that Kingdom in a way that is so livingly real that we – their elders, parents, teachers – must be prepared to learn from them, from their openness, simplicity and trust, and learn in such a way that something of their freshness, spontaneity and brightness comes through to us, becomes part of us. 'I tell you the truth, anyone who will not receive the Kingdom of God like a little child will never enter it at all.'

Every congregation, then, has to find ways of giving the children such a place in its life and fellowship that, at every main gathering of the Lord's people, the girls and boys can be seen, listened to, prayed with. Music and drama give great scope here, especially if the making of the music and the presentation of the drama can be shared between children and adults.

Catholic and Protestant sharing the Peace

The benefits that flowed from the two congregations sharing the same building were quite immense, the greatest being the atmosphere of friendship and trust that gradually developed. Out of this came a series of joint Lenten evening services in which our main concern was to make intercession for the world, and especially for Northern Ireland, where the violence was beginning to escalate at a terrifying speed.

Something happens when Catholics and Protestants come together just to be with one another before the Lord in silent, and sometimes vocal, penitence for all that we have done over many years 'to crucify the Son of God afresh and put him to an open shame'. To make repentance in this unmistakable and locally rooted fashion is to find the words of Jesus at the very beginning of his ministry about the in-breaking Kingdom of God being fulfilled in our own here-and-now experience.

> *After John was put in prison, Jesus went into Galilee, proclaiming the good news of God! 'The time has come,' he said. 'The Kingdom of God is near. Repent and believe the good news.'*
> ~ Mark 1: 14 and 15 (after NIV) ~

Most evenings, these little gatherings ended with our singing Shalom and giving each other the peace as we did so. 'Shalom, my friend, Shalom my friend, Shalom, Shalom.' There is a real sense that, for the people of Scotland, the Lord's Shalom can only be properly shared as Catholics and Protestants make it personally accessible to each other.

A Proper Centre

Two quite serious matters deeply affecting Knightsridge and its future kept coming up at News Time in the Sunday Service and also in the Church Meeting. The first was the need for a more adequate facility to serve as a centre for community life than the existing Sports Pavilion/Family Centre. The Community Council, under the leadership of people like May McCusker and Jim Nicol, worked very hard on this and persuaded the Livingston Development Corporation to make two substantial extensions to the building. This made it possible for young mothers and children, youth groups and senior citizens to have a place to call their own. More than this, May and her friends were successful in interesting the people of Save the Children Fund not only in the Family Centre and its staffing, but also in the Knightsridge Adventure Play Ground.

The main funds for the Adventure Play Ground came through Urban Aid, but Save the Children continued to support, and is still responsible for generous funding. Save the Children Fund has a good name in Scotland, and our experience of teaming up with its workers and officials in Livingston makes this very understandable. Knightsridge would be a much poorer place today but for the supportiveness and generosity of Save the Children Fund.

Eventually, through constant pressure from the Community Council and other Knightsridge groups, a most impressive and commodious centre, Mosswood, was built and opened in 1988. The Development Corporation, the District Council and the Regional Council all had a hand in this notable achievement. People like Ron Muir, the then Regional Councillor, and Maureen Ryce, the District Councillor, have good reason to feel proud of the end result.

My one serious complaint is the seemingly inevitable slowness of local democracy's way of working.

As a result of continuing agitation for a better building, the Livingston Development Corporation organised a high-powered evening meeting in the Knightsridge Family Centre in October 1980. The then Member of Parliament was present, as well as the appropriate representatives from the District Council, the Regional Council, as well as the LDC. About sixty of us came from the community. Speakers from the floor made the case for a 'proper centre' clearly and powerfully enough, but 'the powers that be' on the platform, or at least some of them, were far from being persuaded. The MP insisted that sixty people at a week-night meeting was a particular pointer to the absence of any 'head of steam' in the community itself. He said: 'You have a Community High School up at Deans. You have another Community Centre at Inveralmond in Ladywell. Get on with making the most of these, as I know many in different communities throughout West Lothian would be mighty glad to have the chance of doing.' This was backed by a leading staff member from Deans High School: 'I like the look of this little centre with its shopping precinct. This can meet your basic needs, and for the rest come to us at Deans High.'

I reckoned at the time that these two speeches set back the campaign by something like five years. If the MP and the Deans High teacher had been able to spend some time without their cars, walking about Knightsridge, and had been able to put themselves in the shoes of a young mother with toddlers living in Knightsridge IV, they would have realised that to travel two miles each way to Deans High made such demands on their energy and/or their purse that the prospect was quite prohibitive. How important for people in power, from ministers or priests in the local church, through to Members of Parliament and Ministers of State, to abandon their cars and go walkabout in all their urban communities, especially those where increasing poverty can be doing such damage.

Worthier Surroundings

The other issue concerning us all at this time was the notorious Knightsridge IV area, where space provision had been virtually ignored. The original designer of the area had been given some prestigious architectural award, but from the people living there the only award was the proverbial raspberry. Give the LDC its due, its town planners readily acknowledged the faults and failures in the scheme, and they did quite a bit by way of structural remedial work – but the harshness remained.

Without any authority other than the continuing complaints and my own troubled conscience, I rang the Convenor of Lothian Region's Social Work committee, Mrs Phyllis Herriot, and told her the sorry story of the Knightsridge IV area in Livingston. Immediately she said, 'I'll come out and see the place myself'.

The Convenor was as good as her word. She came to Knightsridge and brought with her a band of officials and Councillors, Eric Milligan, then Convenor of the Council (now Lord Provost of Edinburgh) among them. They spent two hours in the area, met some of the people most deeply affected, made no promises, but undertook to do everything they could to support any moves on the part of LDC to improve matters, and to get rid of the noxious label, 'problem area', from the Knightsridge community.

Some time after this, our Knightsridge Church Council invited Napier College in Edinburgh to send a team of researchers from its Sociology Department to survey the area, and to suggest ways of making the place more socially acceptable to the residents and to the rest of us. This was carried through, and copies of the team's report were sent to the LDC and to Mrs Herriot.

Some of us in Knightsridge were more than half expecting a furious and dismissive response from LDC. Instead the new Housing Manager, David Kelly, expressed genuine appreciation. There and then he set about organising a half-day conference in Napier College with the people responsible for the survey and others, including

Professor David Lindsay, from the College's Sociology Department, and a strong representation from Knightsridge itself.

For me the high point of the conference came near the end when Mrs Donaldson, Head of Knightsridge Nursery School, told of how a child from one of the 'Ways' in the area under discussion was taken ill at school. She took him home and saw him settled with his mother. 'I was upset and angered,' she said, 'not by the state of the home, but by the bleakness, greyness and wretched layout in that particular Way.' Then, turning to the LDC representatives, she said with strong feeling: 'You have no right to consign any child in Livingston to conditions like these.'

I like to think that this powerful plea by Mrs Donaldson at the Napier College Conference was a root cause of the far-reaching renovation work begun by the Development Corporation in its 'Knightsridge Initiative', and of all the benefits that flowed from the resulting rehabilitation of the area.

Three Women of Knightsridge

Margaret Hutchison

Margaret Hutchison had been a hospital matron for many years. She had been widowed and was in indifferent health when she came to live in Morrison Way in Knightsridge, but neither her widow-hood nor her ailments were allowed to dominate her life. Margaret revelled in the challenge of letting a new church be born in her community and readily took on the counsellor's job in her own street.

When she was fit enough, two, sometimes three, afternoons or summer evenings were devoted to door-knocking round her 'patch', and it was here that the indomitable element in her faith was most clearly seen. Her neighbours, or most of them, welcomed these visits, but few at that point showed any active interest in the church or church services.

You could have been forgiven for thinking that her time and energy might have been used to more profitable ends, but that would have been to completely mis-read Margaret's sense of being called to show the Lord's love by sharing her love with the people around her. Her visits were never bare visits. She had listened again and again to her Lord giving his instructions to the seventy missioners: 'When you knock at any house door first say in your heart "Peace be to this house"', and Margaret never went visiting without praying for the people she expected to meet, and afterwards holding them by name in her evening prayers. That kind of visiting, backed by that kind of praying, has the very powers of God's Kingdom in and around it, and several of Margaret's neighbours could and did testify to just that.

Knightsridge was required to find homes for eight refugee Vietnamese families. Margaret learned through her grapevine that the LDC had allocated a house for one family next door to a notoriously 'difficult' household. Immediately, Margaret phoned the housing people at the Corporation Development offices, saying this would be a quite disastrous move. Another house with kindly neighbours was quickly found and the refugee family, through Margaret and others, found welcome and continuing support.

When Margaret in her last long illness was too weak to come to Holy Week services, she would invite her neighbours to come to her home. There they could share the Bible readings for the day and prayers for all the Lord's people, that they might be led in the way of the Cross and find it to be the way of life and peace.

One of the first gifts given to the new Knightsridge congregation was a little framed tapestry made by herself, showing a Bible lying open for everyone to see. Each time the congregation gathers, that simple expression of a believer's faith, so lovingly worked, serves to remind young and old that the word of the Lord can still evoke the kind of love and devotion we saw so clearly in Margaret Hutchison, a love and devotion that can gladden many hearts and brighten many lives.

Fiona Ford

Fiona Ford was quite badly disabled by cerebral palsy. She had been brought up in a deeply Christian home and her faith counted for something very real and positive in her daily life. She studied at Stirling University and took her degree in Sociology.

Fiona fell in love with Michael, himself badly disabled as a result of mugging in a city on the Continent. Friends used to say something like this: 'Of course it's all right, Fiona, to fall in love, but you must not think of marriage.' To this, Fiona would reply: 'In my book, love is about commitment and so is Christian marriage. Michael and I are to be married, and soon.' And they did, in one of the most moving marriage services I have ever officiated at.

'Now, Fiona,' friends began to say, 'you're well and truly married, but you must never think about having a child – that would be far too dangerous.' Fiona, however, soon became pregnant. Relatives, friends, neighbours, shook their heads and waited with growing concern. The baby duly arrived, and all of us in the streets were told of this by the early morning milkman shouting through every letterbox: 'Fiona's had her baby! A girl! They're both great!' The news certainly released a great flood of thankfulness and joy.

Well before the birth of the new baby, Fiona and Michael were sent by the Knightsridge congregation to take part in the annual gathering of the Taizé people, held that year in London. When they returned it was quite evident to everyone that this had been a mountain-top experience for them both, and something of the transfiguring brightness was still about them. They said:

It was quite wonderful. No debating. No arguing. No motions or counter-motions. We prayed with one another. We spoke with one another. We meditated together in silence. We sang new songs, or rather old songs from the Bible in a new way. Something happened to us and everyone else. The Holy Spirit came and took possession of us all in a way that was quite unmistakable and unforgettable.

They did not need to tell us this! We could see it in their faces and hear it in their voices.

One of the features of our mid-week worship in Knightsridge was the input that came, through Fiona and others, from the Monday evening charismatic gathering in St Andrews Catholic Church in Craigshill. Sometimes it was a verse or two from a new song, or a story that someone told, or a fresh recounting of a Bible story. After their Taizé days in London, both Fiona and Michael – especially Fiona – continued to do this in a still more loving, more inspired way, and helped several of us realise more than ever that the 'fellow-ship of the Holy Spirit' seems to take special delight, not only in overcoming age-old man-made barriers, but in helping us to taste and to see the joy of the Lord in a new fullness.

Two things further have to be noted. I could never visit Fiona's home without finding someone else there – a young mother on her own, desperately trying to cope on a social security allowance that would test the ablest manager; a teenager with a drink or drugs problem; an older woman struggling to find her way back to a normal lifestyle after a serious nervous breakdown. This openness of heart made Fiona's caring special, and seemed always to have about it that unforced, unselfconscious quality seldom found any-where, except amongst those who are deeply and personally involved in that fellowship of Holy Spirit, that works by love and has constant prayer as its heart.

Fiona was an active member of her local Labour Party. Her main contribution to policymaking discussions seems to have been her constant insistence that the needs of the hungry peoples of the Third World be given proper place.

One day Fiona went to visit her father in hospital in Glasgow. During that visit she herself took ill and was taken into hospital with a mysterious virus illness. She never recovered. This death, so utterly unexpected, affected everyone in the Knightsridge com-munity, and filled many hearts with anguish and dismay.

The funeral service was held in Daldowie Crematorium, Glasgow on a beautiful Spring morning. The place was packed, with people standing in the aisles. However, what was so remarkable about the service was not anything in the service itself, but in what happened after the benediction and the departure of the ministers. When we returned from the vestry we found, instead of a slowly skailing congregation, everyone was still in their place, and all singing their hearts out in songs, new songs, of praise and thanksgiving. One that I remember particularly, by Dave Bilbrough, was especially appro-priate:

Let there be love shared among us,
Let there be love in our eyes.

Fiona's friends in the Monday evening gathering at St Andrew's Catholic Church in Craigshill, had come in strength to the service in Daldowie and then, having shared as freely and tearfully as the rest of us in the conventional service, began to sing their simple Gospel songs, all telling of a life that is stronger than death, of a life that even in the face of death finds a defiant joy and something to sing about.

When at last the congregation began to move out, I found myself standing in the vestibule greeting people as they passed. One young woman, a leading activist in Fiona's branch of the Livingston Labour Party, stopped. Holding me by the shoulders, she sobbed through her tears: 'Oh minister, all these people have a faith and I have none.' The thought hit me then – even after her death, Fiona's love does stirring work!

Agnes Feeney

Agnes Feeney lived in Barclay Way, Knightsridge, but her place of worship was with the Brethren in the Deans area. She was housebound, and I used to call, not for her sake but for my own.

To talk with Agnes was to realise how much faith and the practice of prayer can do still to lift us out of ourselves and our afflictions, and to allow the kind of laughter that has been described as a 'sudden glory' to brighten our conversation. Whatever topic we were discussing, Agnes would bring it round to the Lord, his loving dealings with us, and his eagerness to help, whatever the need.

Always after we had prayed together for a few moments, I would take my leave with Agnes's gentle blessing ringing in my ears: 'The Lord go with you and make his joy your strength.'

Every time I visited with Agnes Feeney, I was reminded of the person going through a long illness who had an empty chair always at the side of his bed. One day the minister said to him: 'Sandy – you're looking better today.' Sandy, putting his hand on the 'empty' chair, replied: 'Minister – He and I have been gey chief these last few days.' It always seemed to me that the secret of the ambience surrounding this loving child of God lay in her being 'gey chief' with her Lord, all day and every day ....

CHAPTER 9

Iona

FROM early on in my ministry, I learned the worth of visits to Iona, especially for younger people. A group from our Youth Fellowship in Kirkcaldy spent a week on the island at the beginning of the Iona Community's Summer Youth Camps. The young folk returned from Iona late on a Saturday night and came to the service in the church on the Sunday morning. I met up with them outside the church immediately after the service and found them glum and lugubrious in the extreme. 'What's the matter?' I asked. 'Oh,' came the reply, 'it's just terrible to come back to a service like that after worshipping all week in the Abbey.'

As the minister responsible I was not a little nettled, for I had thought the service just finished was as good and lively as any. However I, with many Scottish ministers, had to learn that traditional parish worship – its singings, prayers and preaching – were due for drastic overhaul if our young people were not to turn their backs on us for good and all. Undoubtedly the Iona Community's main contribution to the renewal of Church life in Scotland has been made at this level of daily worship. Here is the kind of worship that encourages personal participation from beginning to end of the service. Whatever else people, and especially young people, are looking for in the Church's worship – being caught up in it is really of the essence. Without that kind of involvement, the entire service cannot but be 'dead in the water' with all its dreichness and heaviness.

In Livingston we aimed to have a group from our own and other parishes spend a week on Iona every year. These visits did much for the people taking part, but they also did a great deal for the parent congregations when these people returned to share something of the community's vision of the 'crown rights of the Redeemer', of the Christ whose Kingdom has as much to do with politics as with the pieties of religion. The Iona challenge to the Churches in any one locality seems to me still to lie in our finding ways of helping one another to hold together, in the ongoing life of these very churches, our commitment to God's justice in the community and the world and our practice of prayer. This especially includes the prayer Jesus taught us to say and to keep on saying: 'Your Kingdom come. Your will be done on earth as it is in heaven.'

My own experience of these visits made me realise that it is the 'uncovenanted blessings' that give them their unique worth. Here are some examples of what I mean.

On most visits we had at least one quite severely disabled person. Bob Steedman, who had multiple sclerosis, came with us on several occasions. Bob, by his genial and good-humoured acceptance of the constant help he needed to negotiate the stairs at the Abbey, and to make his way as far as St Columba's Bay on the Wednesday pilgrimage round the island, made a quite distinctive and remarkable contribution to the worth of the week as an experience of the kind of fellowship the Spirit gives. For Bob himself, these weeks on Iona were the highlight of his year and gave him such a feeling for the renewing powers of the Gospel that he could not bear to lie down to his trouble. He just had to be pushing out in new ventures of discovery by intensive study of Gaelic, German, History, and so on. This eagerness to learn stayed with him to the last.

One year we arrived on Iona to discover that two other groups were our 'partners in learning' – disabled young people from city hospitals and a number of borstal boys from Polmont. All of us were expected to take what part we could in ensuring that the 'differently able' were as mobile as the rest of us. One of the Polmont young men insisted on taking full responsibility for seeing to it that one particular disabled person was properly and constantly looked after. This meant that he shared as fully as possible in all the daily programme's activities, including the pilgrimage right round the island on the Wednesday. On the Thursday evening, the Act of Belief was held in the Abbey. The disabled person let his minder know that he would like to be taken forward to make his own personal commitment to the Lord and his work. For a few moments they debated together whether the minder, who had never in his life, so we imagined, had had two serious thoughts about religion, should do the needful, or should someone else be found? 'Look,' said the borstal boy, 'I have been allowed to look after you every day this week. Why should I stand back at this point?'

In the event, they not only went forward together, but just before the officiating minister came along the row with a Gospel word and blessing for each person making commitment of himself to the Christ and his way, the minder came from standing behind the disabled person's chair and knelt beside his new friend to receive his own word and blessing as well.

For several years the life and soul of the Livingston groups on Iona was David Houston, a retired personnel worker whose home was in East Kilbride. David had little time for the traditional Churches and their ways, but he was a single-minded believer in the Gospel as he understood it and a great-hearted supporter of individuals and movements in which he recognised the authentic Spirit of the Gospel.

On the last day of our week's stay on the island, a day of brilliant sun, we walked together to the North End, sat for a time gazing at the white sands and shimmering waves which were given an almost unearthly brightness by the quality of the light. Without a word David took off his shoes, rolled up his trousers and shirt sleeves, and waded into the water. But it was not just for a paddle. Making a cup of his hands, he started to pour the water over his head and shoulders until he was completely soaked. He said afterwards that he had often done this and always felt spiritually cleansed. Undoubtedly there was something of a true baptism in this action. It certainly reminded me of Temple Gairdner, the famous Anglican missionary, who used to speak of 'Iona and its holy cleanness'.

Somehow the young, and the not so young, find something in the place, in its people, and in the worship they share, that speaks to them of wholeness and gives them living experience of its reality.

PART THREE
A Grassroots Spirituality

If the Church can become a praying Church,
it may be of some real use.

~ Revd Brian Hardy ~

CHAPTER 10

The Message

IT hardly needs saying that for nurture and testing, directing and re-directing our spiritual life, the Bible is our first and greatest resource. The Creation story; the faith and faithfulness of the patriarchs – Abraham, Isaac and Jacob; the commitment and staunchness of Moses the liberator, teacher and leader of his people; the courage and passionate conviction of the prophets declaring with such searching clarity the way of God and the justice of God – all this along with the psalmists' and Job's personal experience of the Lord who finds us in the wilderness, so often of our own making, and, in his own time and by his own paths, leads us to still waters and green pastures. Yes, all can indeed be food and drink for every soul on pilgrimage to the Eternal City. Set alongside this the Gospel of Jesus and his Apostles, and we have for our taking nothing less than 'bread of the world in mercy broken, wine of the soul in mercy shed'.

This and much more is certainly true of the Bible, but it is also true that the Bible is a book and therefore its significance for every people in every age depends on how we approach it and how we interpret it. For us in our time with its endless wars, its mammoth murderings and cruelties and the silent holocaust of Third World hunger, we need from the Bible and 'the people of the Book' above everything else, a message that carries within it the secret of reconciliation, of living community, of God-given powers for loving.

In one of the later documents of the early Church, the letters of John, there is an excellent summary of the essentials for a Christian's faith today:

This is the message we have heard from him and have to share with you:
God is light. In him there is no darkness at all ....
If we walk in the light as he is in the light, we have fellowship with
one another.

And the blood of Jesus, his son, cleanses us from sin.
~ 1 John 1: 5-7 (NIV) ~

The God in whom Christians believe, the God in whom is all our hope for a better day, a better world, is no longer hidden away in the dark shadowlands of superstition and fear and ever-threatening terror. God is near, God is with us, as inescapably as the daylight on which all our life depends from first to last.

The light that shines in Orkney is the same light that shines on the Scottish Borders. The light that shines in Europe is essentially the same light as shines in Africa and the Far East. The God whom the Gospel proclaims is the God who is there, equally, searchingly, life-givingly there for the people of the South as much as for the people of the North. In the economy of the Gospel there can be no such thing as a 'Third World'. There is one world, God's world, with God's light shining in it throughout to make us realise that we are all nations, races, peoples – members one of another.

If one member suffers, all humankind has, in one way or another, to share that suffering.

For the making of a new world order, it is this kind of fundamental belief that must take centre stage and begin to give increasing numbers of us a fresh awareness of the part we are called to play in the drama of life's conflicts, confusions and grim mysteries. All the world is indeed a stage, but a stage that belongs to God. It is his light that allows us see properly the different parts we have to play and the people with whom we have to play them out. In a strange, paradoxical way, this God is sharing the action and is in some ultimate sense the director and producer of it all.

The World of Nature

God is the light that gives life and growth and beauty and colour to the natural world.

For far too long the Churches in this and other countries seem to have been possessed by a dumb devil – a silent, destructive indifference – so far as our responsibility for the natural world is concerned. With the exception of a few lonely prophetic voices in the nineteenth and early twentieth centuries, little was heard from the pulpits of Britain, Europe, America on the urgency of the need to find a real reverence for all God's creation just because it is his and never ours, never mankind's to exploit, pulverise, pollute as he may determine.

One of the most hopeful developments in this century is the increasing concern amongst people, especially young people, of all countries that we change direction here before it is too late and this fragile earth be swept finally into the abyss.

The Earth Summit held in Rio, Brazil in 1992 has given clear rulings on how we can go forward, but these rulings have yet to find a foremost place in the activities and discussions of most local churches and other groups at the grassroots of our common life.

Practical guidance and help are available for us in Scotland through the Catholic Commission on Justice and Peace, as well as through the Action of Churches Together in Scotland (ACTS) Commission on Justice, Peace and the Integrity of Creation.

If our experience is anything to go by, children and young people are our strongest allies in working for the 'greening' of the environment locally and worldwide. They, perhaps more than anyone, can help us all make the Bible's affirmation with a new simplicity and conviction: 'The world belongs to the Lord/The earth and its people are his' (Psalm 24: 1, *Iona Community Worship Book*, p 17).

The following quotation, from the World Council of Churches publication *Redeeming The Creation,* is a powerful reminder of our calling as Christians:

Our churches themselves must be places where we learn anew what it means that God's covenant extends to all creatures, by rediscovering the eco-centric dimension of the Bible. This means a modest material lifestyle that loves and treats the earth gently, as God does. At the same time we should include the material elements in our celebrations and praise the cosmic symphony the Spirit is continually composing. As we do so, we should cultivate a penitential attitude for the sins committed against nature and nurture compassion for the beings we harm (Philippians 2: 1-5). We should fashion relations of inclusion and reconciliation between the sexes, between races, cultures and peoples, maintaining a posture of blessed anointing before each being and the whole body of beings. For

*remember, dear sisters and brothers, we are the body of Christ and mem-
bers of the cosmic temple of God. Let us pray during this Pentecost
season, then, for the Holy Spirit to come upon us afresh. Let us cry out
with all our being, 'Come Holy Spirit, Renew the whole Creation'.*

Joy in the Lord

Scottish congregations, Catholic and Protestant, also need to take
the following from the Gospel – God is light; and flatness, dullness,
dreariness in life and worship all belong to the darkness that the
Good News of Jesus and the Resurrection has scattered for ever.

The main part of the secret of commending the Gospel to others,
especially to our children, lies in the reality of the joy they see
and feel amongst the people of God. This, far more than eloquent
preaching, liturgical correctness, fine music, or splendid architec-
ture, exerts magnetic power amongst the un-churched. Sometimes
this joy finds expression in uninhibited movement, song and dance.
Whatever our personal preferences may be, we have to recognise
that such expressions of powerful emotions have always had their
place from New Testament times onward. Most of us still find
speaking with tongues baffling, but we cannot deny that Paul
recognised it as an authentic outpouring of a person's or a people's
rejoicing in the salvation made theirs through the Gospel.

Let none of us be dismissive of the Charismatic Movement. Its
people have so much to share with the rest of us about the joy of the
Lord bringing a Spirit-worked strength to sweep away the barriers
that shut us out from one another and keep us entombed in the sad
sepulchres of our festering histories. So often I hear from amongst
the Charismatics, as I hear from few others, the voice of the Lord
calling to ministers, priests, people in the traditional Churches in
all their staidness and separateness: 'Lazarus, come forth.'

In John 15, Jesus says: 'I have told you all this so that my joy may
be in you and that your joy may be complete.' This joy can make
itself known in all kinds of ways – in the fervour we bring to the
Lord's praises in our hymns and psalms and spiritual songs, as well as
in the way we greet our fellow Christians in the church gathering
itself, and especially in the way we look at, speak with, respond to,

the children and young people sharing the worship. Increasing numbers of churches make a space in their main services for the congregation to give one another the peace by shaking hands, or hugging one another, or kissing one another. This simple action does undoubtedly help many to realise that the Church is first of all a living, loving fellowship in the Spirit. Declaring this in the giving and receiving of the peace can release throughout the congregation a deepening sense of belonging to the Lord and to one another. The joy that goes with that is irrepressible and unmistakable.

We must never imagine that the joy the Spirit brings is confined to church gatherings and church people. Our neighbour along the street, who would perhaps never think to darken a church door, is meant to benefit from the joy given in the Gospel, not in any fussy over-forceful way, but in a friendliness and openness on our part and in a readiness to make space in our prayers for him and his.

I love my Lord
As he loves me
Merrily.
I feel his kisses
In the breeze
And so
I carve his name
On trees.
Why not?
Two thousand years
Misunderstood
He needs my kisses
In the wood
A lot.   ~ Source not known ~

Fellowship

If we walk in the light, as he is in the light, we have fellowship with one another.

To walk in the light has a tremendous consequence – that we have fellowship with one another. Where fellowship among Christ's people is lost for whatever fine-sounding reasons, we have somewhere, somehow, turned our backs on the light and are really floundering in the dark and cold of a Gospel-denying religiosity.

Saint Paul writes strongly in 1 Corinthians 1: 10-17 (NIV):

> *I appeal to you, brothers, in the name of our Lord Jesus Christ, that all of you agree with one another so that there may be no divisions among you and that you may be perfectly united in mind and thought.*

Look at any Scottish town or city. It is not just that divisions are palpably evident in almost every other street, but that ministers and priests, people and their leaders, seem to find these divisions perfectly acceptable and in no sense a flagrant contradiction of the heart and soul of our faith, a denial of Christ and a blockage to the Spirit's working.

Look at the society to which we all belong in Britain – so fragmented, so grey and despair-making for many, so wrapped round in luxury for others;

Our education for so many of our children poverty-stricken and repressive;

Our work life so blighted by mass unemployment that the abilities and potential skills of millions are being abandoned to the rust heap.

I believe that the Gospel of God's justice and God's healing is for us all – people in politics, people in industry and business, people in the professions – as we try to face up to the world of our time and its quite overwhelming needs. If the Church is to be able to give reality to the nature – and urgency – of the Gospel's input here, it has to find ways of breaking free from its ancient, hard institutional rigidities and self-concern and be ready to lose itself – or seeming to lose itself – in the multi-cultural, multi-faith societies that are such an inescapable feature of every nation's life in our western world.

It was Philip Potter, formerly General Secretary of the World Council of Churches, who said this: 'In a world in which the language of faith has lost meaning for lack of translation into life, the acting out of God's kind of sharing announces as no words can the good news of Christ to human kind.'

Cleansing through the Crucified

And the blood of Jesus Christ, his Son, cleanses us from sin.

It is always tempting for any new movement imbued and driven by a strong enthusiasm to imagine that for itself and its members sin is something that has been sloughed off and left behind for ever. We have a work to do, a world to conquer, tidings of new life to share. Sin with its stealth and its poison, its devouring jealousies and ice-cold superiorities and indifference – all this belongs to the old devil-ridden order, done away for good and all at Calvary. Sin? Think nothing of it.

There is big, liberating truth in all that, but it is not the whole truth nor anything like it.

> *I never took my neighbour's life,*
> *My neighbour's purse I never stole*
> *But God have mercy on my soul*
> *For all the good I have not done.*
> *O unattempted loveliness!*
> *O costly valour never won.*   ~ source not known ~

It is not the mediocrities but the saints, and the farthest ben at that, who are most profoundly aware of their own sin and sinfulness. It is these same saints who help us to see in the Crucified not just one who was himself sinless, but one who so identifies himself with the rejects, the outcasts, the failures and the sinners that he is able to bring to them, bring to us, the release and cleansing of a love so amazing, so divine, that only God, Maker of heaven and earth, could be its presence and its power.

The writer to the Hebrews puts it like this (12: 18-24, NIV): 'You have not come to a mountain that can be touched and that is burning with fire, to darkness, gloom and storm .... But you have come to the city of the living God ... to Jesus the mediator of a new covenant and to the sprinkled blood that speaks a better word than the blood of Abel.' The blood of Abel speaks of resentment, jealousy, hate and murder and of the innocent suffering helplessly at the hands of the guilty. The blood of Jesus speaks of the suffering victim so assimilating into himself the resentment, jealousy and murderous hate that they become part of an atoning love, a transforming, reconciling, new-creating love.

To the Crucified we can bring our own sins, the sins that we know and the sins that we know not. He, quite uniquely, can deal with them because he died for them. Here, in the Crucified, is a love that helps us to see these persistent, wretched sins 'nailed to his cross, buried in his tomb and remembered no more against us'. It was Saint Augustine who cried: 'O most blessed sin that brought me to know the most blessed Saviour.'

To the Crucified we can bring our sinning selves. The good that I want to do, I cannot do. The evil that I don't want to do, that I do. O wretched man that I am! Who can deliver me from such a morass as this? The Crucified can because, knowing me for what I truly am, he yet loves me with a love stronger than the sin in me, stronger than death itself, a love that will never let me go and never let me be.

To the Crucified we can bring this world of ours in all its be-devilment, anguish and brokenness. In the very next chapter – 1 John 2: 1 and 2 – Jesus is described as the Righteous One, the One who has an all-consuming passion for God's justice in the world, because he himself is the very justice of God come amongst us. 'He is the atoning sacrifice for our sins; and not only for ours, but for the sins of the whole world.'

In the face of Auschwitz and its unspeakable atrocities; in the face of Northern Ireland and its wanton killings; Bosnia and its 'ethnic cleansing'; Rwanda and its mass murders; in the face of Sudan, Somalia, Angola … their people ravaged by war, ravaged by famine – in the face of all this, what can the people of God do but throw themselves down at the feet of the Crucified and cry out to him and keep crying out to him:

Lamb of God, you take away the sins of the world
Take away our sin
Lamb of God, you take away the sins of the world
Take away our sin
Lamb of God, you take away the sins of the world
Bring us all into your peace.

CHAPTER 11

Ways and Means

FOR people seeking the way in Scotland, there is another Bible passage – this time from the Gospel story itself – that is of quite fundamental importance for our faith and daily living.

In Luke 11: 1-4, Jesus and his disciples are on their last journey to Jerusalem. The disciples, noticing perhaps that prayer is taking an ever larger part in Jesus' day, make this straightforward request: 'Lord, teach us to pray.'

The answer Jesus gives is not a sermon on prayer and its different aspects, but an actual prayer that they have to make their own and keep using throughout the day, throughout the week:

When you pray, say:
'Father,
your name be honoured
your kingdom come
your will be done on earth as it is in heaven
Give us each day our daily bread.
Forgive us our sins,
for we also forgive everyone who sins against us
And lead us not into temptation
But deliver us from the evil one.'

'When you pray, say: "Father".' The word 'father' is key to all our Lord's thinking and teaching about God. He believed in God as maker of heaven and earth, the Eternal, the Almighty, the Ruler and Judge of all humankind. However, the central and controlling truth about God, for Jesus, undoubtedly lies in his strong fatherly care for all his children and for all his creatures. If the members of the Churches can help one another to keep this to the forefront of all their thinking, teaching, planning, they are not likely to lose their way or lose their courage. Even when there is so much all around that seems to stand in flat contradiction of such a seemingly naïve faith, our constant use of the one word arrow prayer, 'Father', can do a great deal to prevent us being completely overwhelmed by the hurts and contradictions of life. Light may not break there and then, but sufficient grace is given for us to go on waiting and looking and praying in hope, in 'trembling' hope, very often in 'hope against hope'.

> O Israel, look to the Lord,
> As those who watch for the morning.
> O Israel, look to the Lord,
> For with the Lord is love unfailing
> And great is his power to set people free.   ~ Psalm 130 ~

Belief in this unfailing love – in all its fatherly, motherly, filial reality – is positively affirmed every time we direct the mind to God in using the one name Jesus taught us to use: 'Father' ... 'Our Father'.

Giving God His Place

No one can read the Lord's Prayer without being struck by the way it centres on God: not on our needs or the world's needs, but on God, on the honouring of his name, on the coming of his Kingdom and the doing of his will. So often we church people give the impression that our faith amounts to little more than this: 'God is indeed a good fellow just waiting to be called in when everyone and everything else have failed.' But God is not that kind of a good fellow and is at no one's beck and call. What we have to share with our children, and with one another, is the good news that God in his love comes before all, is first and last, the end-all and be-all for everyone and everything.

When an expert in the law tested Jesus with this question, 'Teacher, which is the greatest commandment in the law?', Jesus immediately replied, 'Love the Lord your God with all your heart and with all your soul and with all your mind. This is the first and greatest commandment' (Matthew 22: 36-38).

It was Dubchek of Czechoslovakia who used to plead for socialism 'with a human face'. For his persistence he was banished to the wilderness. For many people the most distinctive and wonderful thing that Jesus has done for them is to give God a human face, the face of a good and loving father whose love is seen most clearly, most searchingly, when it is being rejected, despised, crucified. Here is love – not ours for him, but *his* for *us*. Our love, never very strong, never very deep, derives all its meaning, all its worth and effectiveness, from this other love that so mysteriously surrounds us, puts up with us and, from time to time, allows us to glimpse in him and in some of his servants quite unspeakable glimmerings of glory.

Your Kingdom come
Your will be done
on earth as it is in heaven

Quite astounding! One highly suspect leader, banished from the synagogues, regarded by the priestly establishment as subversive of the great Temple and its worship, with a rag-tag band of men and women gathered from the highways and byways of Galilee and Judea – here they are in the wilds of Palestine, having no social standing, no political programme and nothing like the military might of the Roman legions everywhere in evidence around them. What are they being taught to pray for, to look for, to live for? Nothing less than the transforming of life in all the world by the coming of God's Kingdom and the fulfilment of God's purposes. Right from the beginning the world was their parish and they are not the least apologetic for their own seeming insignificance in face of their declared aims, so astonishing in their sweep and magnitude.

George MacLeod of the Iona Community used to be fond of referring to the early Celtic missionaries, whose one ambition was expressed in the words: 'Foreign mould over us at the last.' They could feel like this and speak like this, because they had come to see all the world as beloved by God and belonging to God. For a Christian to die on the march in some distant land, among an alien people, is simply to affirm that that land and that people are God's, that his Kingdom is among them and will continue among them to reveal his judging, serving, reconciling love. 'God was in

Christ reconciling the world to himself ... and has committed to us the Gospel of reconciliation' (2 Corinthians 5: 19).

The Kingdom that surely comes

When we pray 'Your Kingdom come', we are looking for something far bigger and more important than adding to the membership of any Church. Look at the different pictures Jesus draws to help us realise the nature of the Kingdom. The Kingdom of God is like a grain of mustard seed, so tiny as to seem quite insignificant, but what powers of growth it holds like a piece of leaven hidden in a great lump of heavy dough. What a transforming work that leaven can do! It is like a shepherd seeking out his one lost sheep, like a housewife searching for a lost coin, like a father waiting, longing, watching for the return of his wayward son.

Clearly the Kingdom has to do with all life and affects every aspect of it: the life of nature; the life of nations; home life; work life; community life; the quality of the schooling provided for our children; the kind of solidarity that transcends the havoc-wreaking divisions of poverty and wealth, of racism, sexism, ageism. To be praying the Kingdom means rejoicing in the exceeding diversity and richness of its life, and to be supporting one another in the inescapable conflict with everything and everyone working against the life-saving, life-enhancing powers of God in his Kingdom. One German sociologist of religion suggests that anyone who 'takes the message of Jesus seriously in any culture, even a so-called Christian culture, ultimately becomes an outsider'. When, however, the outsiders in any culture are in touch with one another through the Spirit of God, they themselves can and do become 'the seed growing secretly', the leaven of a richer, more inclusive culture.

The wording of this part of the Lord's Prayer is important. Jesus does not say 'pray: Father help us to build your Kingdom' – although for most of the time our deeply ingrained Western activism makes us understand it in this way. But Jesus wants us to grasp and live the faith that the initiative for a more just way of living, any worthwhile move towards a kindlier, more peaceful world, must have the Lord God for author. Therefore whatever else we do we must, from first to last, be looking to him, be prepared for new leading from him, be ready to help one another to make fresh ventures in loving obedience to the vision he has given us in Jesus. The Gospel for ourselves and for our world is that the Kingdom is God's and that he alone can give it life and reality amongst us and he does this so often in the most unexpected ways and through the most unlikely people.

> *Father: Your name be honoured*
> *Your Kingdom come*
> *Your will be done*
> *On earth as it is in heaven*

If there is to be peace in Britain and in Ireland, if there is to be peace in Europe where murderous 'ethnic cleansing' has brought such shame on us all, if there is to be even the beginnings of peace for our world in the new millennium, then this prayer for the coming of God's Kingdom must be seen as the one dynamic that matters for all our living, thinking, proclaiming.

Bread for Our Bodies

At this point in the Lord's Prayer I like to pause and draw breath. This next part has to do with our personal needs if we are to count, as believing disciples are meant to count, for this Kingdom that Jesus brings.

> *Give us today our daily bread.*

It is often said that Christianity is the most materialist of all religions. Certainly Jesus not only taught us to pray for our daily bread, but he himself fed the hungry out in the wilds and laid it down in the great and terrible parable of judgment that what we do, or fail to do, about the hungry reveals what we truly are in God's sight and the reality or unreality in our profession of righteousness, our concern for justice in the world.

I was hungry. What did you do about that? In as much as you did it or did it not to one of the least of these, my brothers and sisters, you did it or did it not to me.   ~ Matthew 25 ~

We have just been praying for God's will to be done on earth as perfectly as it is done in heaven. So when we go on to pray for our daily bread, our asking has to do not just with ourselves and our own family's need, but with all God's hungry children in every land and amongst every people. The devastating fact that every nine seconds a child in the Third World dies of hunger, or of hunger-related diseases, is such a dreadful indictment not primarily of governments, economists, politicians, but of the people of God taught two thousand years ago how to pray and say – 'Give us today our daily bread.'

An African Christian made this prayer:

I saw a child today, Lord, who will not die tonight,
harried into hunger's grave. He was bright and full of
life because his father has a job and feeds him.
But somewhere, everywhere, ten thousand life lamps
will go out and not be lit again tomorrow.
Lord, teach me my sin. Amen.

Teach me my sin in the way I have been playing games – Mickey Mouse games – with this prayer taught by Christ Jesus on the way to his Cross. Teach me, too, how my praying can release within myself, and in all the world, redemptive powers of healing love.

Bread for Our Souls

Forgive us the wrongs we have done
For we forgive everyone who has wronged us.

I can remember reading a novel by C. P. Snow, called *The Masters*. A new principal for one of the university's colleges is to be chosen from several applicants, and those responsible for making the final choice are agreeing how impossibly difficult it is to read with any

accuracy the true mind and character of any other person. The
narrator says something like this:

> *When we look into our own hearts we cannot but be appalled and have
> to find ways of forgiving ourselves if we are to get along with the business
> of living.*

There is an honesty here that we all instantly recognise. The
depths of evil in our own hearts is no invention of the moralist or the
way-out 'evangelical'. If, however, our only answer for this profound,
persistent need lies in finding ways to forgive ourselves, we are
indeed of all men the most miserable. Human beings are not noted
for their ability to forgive themselves. Witness Shakespeare's Lady
Macbeth trying desperately to get the blood stains off her hands,
crying out in anguish, '… not all the perfumes of Arabia can ever
sweeten this little hand …. Out, out, damned spot'.

Jesus teaches his people to say simply: 'Forgive us, Father, for
we forgive.' We are able to carry about with us a truly forgiving, a
genuinely accepting attitude to one another because God in Jesus
has allowed us to hear the Gospel word: 'Come in peace. Your sins,
even yours, are forgiven.' It is the realisation, sudden or gradual,
that 'the love that moves the sun and the other stars' is the same love
that comes when all the doors of our defences are bolted and barred
for fear, for fear of being found out in our emptiness, confusion,
pretentiousness and cringing cowardice, and lets us hear the word
of healing brought out from the black dark of Calvary's anguish,
'Peace be to you'.

It is this realisation that frees us up inside for loving and being
loved in a way that is different. I cannot see how any love, and certainly no married love, can keep its freshness and joy unless at back
of it there is the forgiving love of the Father for his children. I
cannot see how family love can survive the slings and arrows of
outrageous behaviour on the part of parents towards each other,
towards their children, on the part of teenagers towards their home
and family, without the acknowledgment of a love that is able to
forgive and to accept forgiveness because the living God is in it.

It is told of the artist Rembrandt that when he painted his last
canvas his only possessions were the clothes he was wearing and the

materials he was using. In these harsh and sordid conditions he takes for the subject of his last painting not people in their meanness and blindness, but Jesus' parable of the Prodigal Son. Many claim that art had never produced before, and has never reproduced since, such expressive beauty as this man, in crushing poverty, was able to put into the hands of the Father laid on the stooping shoulders of his boy who has come home.

In the midst of hurt, indifference and overwhelming loveless-ness, this inspired artist is proclaiming his final testimony – that at the heart of all reality is forgiving, welcoming, redeeming love.

Father, forgive us for we forgive.

Reckoning with the Powers of Evil

Lead us not into temptation but deliver us from evil.

The besetting sin for women and men enthused and strengthened by the Spirit to proclaim the Kingdom, heal the sick and drive out demons, was to imagine that they themselves were quite invulner-able and could go on sweeping all before them. Jesus counters this by giving, for the final part of the prayer his friends have to say and keep on saying, the plea that they will never be nakedly exposed to the Tempter's power as the Lord himself was at the very beginning of his mission.

The 'Series III Order for Holy Communion' in the Anglican Church has a very helpful translation of the Lord's prayer:

Do not bring us to the time of trial
but deliver us from evil

Do not bring us to a time of severe testing, for our faith at best is 'crumbly stuff'. Always the one saving hope for any of us must lie in a simple readiness to take our own self-trust, self-love, self-seek-ing with all the demonic subtleties of these strong urges and let the Lord deal with them, expose them and break their hold on us.

My grace is sufficient for you for my strength is made perfect in weak-ness.

The best comment on this part of the Lord's Prayer is in George Macdonald's little pray-poem:

When I look back upon my life nigh spent,
Nigh spent though still the feeble stream flows on
I more of follies than of sins repent,
Less for offence than love's shortcomings moan.
With self, O Father, leave me not alone,
Leave not the beguiler with the beguiled.
Besmirched and ragged, Lord, take back thine own:
A fool I bring thee to be made a child.

When we have been trampled down and broken by the Tempter's power, we are never abandoned or consigned to the trash heap. 'God's gifts and call are without repentance', and and he is able to give us a new kind of wholeness that can make us count in a more telling way especially with and for the people who feel themselves the most put down, the most excluded, the most sorely tried in all the world.

The spirit that imbues this prayer that Jesus wants us to use continually, is very clearly expressed in the story of America's Martin Luther King.

His widow Coretta King, in *My Life with Martin Luther King*, tells how, as a child of four, Martin was out with his father in the main shopping street of their home town. They called in at a shoe shop and sat down in the front seats. The attendant said, politely enough, 'If you will move to the seats at the back, I shall be glad to serve you.'

'Daddy' King's temper flared up: 'You will wait on us here, please.'

The attendant replied: 'I am not allowed to do that.'

So Daddy King took Martin's hand and strode out of the store. As they walked down the street, Daddy King rumbled fiercely in his deep voice: 'I don't care how long I have to live with this thing, I shall never accept it. I'll go on fighting it till I die ….

Nobody can make a slave of you, Martin, if you never think like a slave.'

You don't need to be an educational psychologist to realise what a profound and lasting influence such an incident and such words must have had on this child's outlook and beliefs.

Many years later, when Martin Luther King had become the recognised leader of the Civil Rights movement to secure equality and justice for the black people of the United States, terrible race riots broke out in the Kings' home town of Alabama. In one of these rampages the Kings' home was bombed. The black people were shocked and angry and waiting in their hundreds for the signal to set about the enemy.

Standing on the steps of his bombed out home, Martin Luther King shouted out for all to hear: 'If blood is to flow in the streets of Alabama tonight, let it be our blood.'

For the Kingdom and the power and the glory are yours. Father, Son and Holy Spirit, one God, blessed and blessing for ever.

CHAPTER 12

Learning to bear the Beams of Love

A LONG with the Bible, two books have helped Elizabeth and myself more than I can say to give shape and depth to our daily prayers, particularly our intercessions.

The first of these is the *Iona Community Worship Book* (no publication date), especially its prayers for Peace and Justice set out on pages 37-38 of the *ICWB*. Here is one example of how to use the prayers in the book (the entire week is listed below in Appendix 2, page 146):

★ ★ ★

On Fridays we have to pray for:

Those who help us to celebrate
Artists, music makers and composers, writers, children, friends —

In this last, we make a personal plea for writers like George Mackay Brown of Orkney, searching for ever more effective ways in poetry, drama, novels and short stories, to give glimpses of a life, a love and a 'terrible beauty' so utterly different from the rough and tumble of our everyday living, but without which our days here can be one dimensional and empty of any meaning beyond that conferred by the 'bitch-goddess' success.

Children —

Our own and our neighbours' children. Their parents, their teachers in schools for children with special needs, in nursery, primary and secondary schools. [Here we need to seek help from one another as Protestant and Catholic members of the local community to see if we can find more supportive ways of expressing a genuine solidarity with those at the 'chalk face', especially in our secondary schools. Many of these are the true 'pain-bearers' for our society.]

The Unity of the Church –

For the fresh experience of unity given us in the Livingston Ecumenical Parish; for recent exciting developments in Catholic/Protestant relationships here; and for beckonings to a fuller unity affecting our relations with people of other faiths and the people of our secular communities.

> Collect: *God to enfold us, God to surround us*
> *God in our speaking, God in our thinking*
> *God in our life, God in our lips*
> *God in our souls, God in our hearts*
> *O Holy Spirit of God.*

★ ★ ★

These prayers for justice and peace seem to me to be a vital filling up and filling out of the Lord's prayer: Your Kingdom come. Your will be done on earth.

All of us in the churches must be deeply thankful to the Iona Community for helping us in this way to give a large and significant place in our daily prayers to the justice and peace issues of our time.

The other book from which Elizabeth and I keep deriving so much benefit is the World Council of Churches *With All God's People. The New Ecumenical Prayer Cycle.* What we are being helped to do here is not simply to ask blessing for this country and that, 'but also to understand, to stand alongside, and to pray in solidarity with, our fellow Christians around the world'. The entire world is covered in one year. A week is devoted to a nation or group of nations, and in the space of that one week we are told the essentials of the country's story, including the religious situation there, given grounds for thankfulness for special gifts and achievements, and helped to appreciate the most pressing needs that have to be the burden of our intercessions.

In Week 10 there are two samples of prayers – first for Ireland, then for the United Kingdom – given on pages 76 and 80 of the *Ecumenical Prayer Cycle*.

Lord Jesus Christ, you are the way of peace.
Come into the brokenness of our lives and our land
with your healing love.
Help us to be willing to bow before you in true repentance,
and to one another in real forgiveness.
By the fire of your Holy Spirit, melt our hard hearts
and consume the pride and prejudice which separate us.
Fill us, O Lord, with your perfect love which casts
out fear and bind us together in that unity which you
share with the Father and the Holy Spirit.

[Emerging out of the movement of charismatic renewal, this prayer is used in both the Republic and Northern Ireland.]

Lord God, we thank you
For calling us into the company
Of those who trust in Christ
And seek to obey his will.
May your Spirit guide and strengthen us
In mission and service to your world;
For we are strangers no longer
But pilgrims together on the way to your Kingdom.

[Prayer for the inter-church process, by Jamie Wallace.]

★ ★ ★

On Sunday mornings, before going out to join in the prayers and praises of the church, Elizabeth and I like to remember by name 'those who died on the march', and who had brought to us and to many others a living breath of the Spirit. Most of them were our own close personal friends, but all of them are alive and with us still in the mystery. As they now walk with Christ in light, so our remembering them allows something of that light to shine just a little bit more brightly around us, within us.

And when the strife is fierce, the warfare long,
Steals on the ear the distant triumph song
And hearts are brave again
And arms are strong …

That They may be One

Wherever we start in the search for unity – unity in the world, unity in the Church – however many conferences, study sessions, action schemes, prayer weeks we take part in – always but always, we are drawn to the Upper Room in Jerusalem and into that strange prayer of our Lord for his people, a prayer that has more resonance of the eternities than any other in the Gospel story.

Here in the Upper Room, amidst all his teaching on himself as 'the way, the truth and the life', on his being the true vine, his Father the gardener, his disciples the fruit-bearing branches, amidst his words about that peace of his that the world can neither give nor take away – Jesus does four things of quite special significance:

– He gives the new commandment: 'Love one another, as I have loved you';
– He institutes the Sacrament of Holy Communion;
– He washes his disciples' feet;
– He prays for his believing followers, then and now, 'that they all may be one'.

We cannot be reminded too often that unity is not an optional extra to be taken up when everything else has been dealt with. This unity for which Jesus prays, has to penetrate and permeate every part of our life as Christians.

It is those who are committed, body and soul, to loving one another as Christ loves us, who can truly and deeply know, through their own emptiness and need, that unity is of the essence of being true Church of God in and for his world.

It is those who keep on sharing the Lord's bread and cup in Sacrament, who come to discover the fellowship-creating powers of the Gospel coming alive in and through themselves.

It is those who are brought to their knees, 'serving as though they were slaves', who are ready for the oneness the Lord wants us to have, the Lord says we *must* have, if we are to count in any way that matters for the world and its coming to faith.

All this, as it relates to us and our calling as Christians, has been movingly set out by Jeanne Hendrickse writing out of the old South Africa some years ago.

— *Don't get involved with unity, don't get involved with growing together into unity unless your bones, heart, soul, your whole being cry out for unity.*
— *Don't get involved with human cries of pain, separation, loneliness ... the travail of an earth being raped of its resources.*
— *Don't get involved with injustice, liberation, human rights, hunger, oppression, dignity, unity of churches, understanding, reconciliation, peace.*
— *Don't get involved, unless your whole being cries with Christ for justice, love, humanness, unity, peace.*
— *BUT if you dare, dare to get involved.*
~ Ecumenical Review, vol. 31 no. 1, 1979 ~

The Glory that is different

Just before moving out to Gethsemane and all that lies beyond, Jesus turns from addressing his disciples to addressing the Father. The burden of what the disciples hear, *overhear,* in this prayer is that they be brought into that unity of life and love that the Father himself has with the Son in the communion of the Holy Spirit: 'I have given them the glory that you gave me, that they may be one as we are one' (John 17: 22).

The unity, the only kind of unity that can count powerfully for the world and all its people, has its source not in human ideas, inventions, dreams, but in the God who is Father, Son and Holy Spirit, and who, through Christ the Crucified, makes us sharers of the divine glory, of the very love that is the Spirit's presence and power in our lives and in the life of the Church.

To give the healing of our divisions the urgency and priority, the Gospel demands means recognising and helping one another to to recognise that our calling is indeed to watch with Christ through his agony and bloody sweat in Bosnia, in Rwanda, in the humiliating harshness of Scotland's sectarian displays, and all that lies at back of it.

> *May they be brought to complete unity to let the world know that you sent me.* ~ John 17: 23 ~

God so loved the world that he gave his Son, Jesus of Nazareth, not just to teach and heal and serve, but to suffer, to die and come back from the dead, that the hearts and minds of people everywhere may be opened up to the love that God is waiting to shed abroad in new fullness of healing power.

Jean Vanier, founder of the L'Arche movement for mentally handicapped people, writes of what he himself has discovered of the divine love.

> *The more I deepen the essence of my faith in that love which springs from the heart of God, the more it helps me understand the sufferings, the deep call, the crying out of the human being. And the closer I come to people in their humanity, listening to them and sensing their needs, the more I am confirmed in my faith in Jesus and the essence of his teaching.*

That Jesus said – that Jesus *says* …

> *I have given them the glory that you gave me that they may be one as we are one.*

EPILOGUE

*

by Brian Hardy

IT is, of course, easy to idealise the early years in Livingston New Town. They were in reality anything but easy, not least because of the relentless growth of the population. But as new housing areas were developed, the manner and the method of provision by the churches in Ladywell St Paul's, Dedridge (The Lanthorn), Knightsridge and Carmondean drew on the experience gained in Craigshill and on the vision which had fired it. The transition from the Livingston Ecumenical Experiment to the Livingston Ecumenical Parish has demanded much from all who have participated in it. James himself would perhaps have suspected that the churches in Livingston were becoming 'institutionalised' – a phenomenon which he would have regarded with suspicion if not with horror, for he was never slow in claiming, and jealously guarding, his freedoms!

In Livingston, as elsewhere, things begun with zeal, energy and enthusiasm can encounter periods in which the hard slog has to continue with little apparent inspiration to undergird it. The 'ecumenical experiment' has been at times a goldfish bowl into which observers have gazed with a mixture of wonder and per-plexity; and at other times it has had to bear fierce criticism and resentment. But the very intensity of the responses to Livingston from within the Churches must mean that the underlying concepts are perceived to present the Churches with an agenda, a way of being the Church. The approval by the General Assembly of the Church of Scotland in 1997 of a scheme to establish a single Ecu-menical Parish with at present five congregational centres and a team of at least three stipendiary ministers, may be seen as a move by the Churches to 'own' all that Livingston has struggled to achieve. The vision still remains to be fulfilled, but it has not been quenched.

7 August 1997

Livingston
A Regional City in the Lothians, Scotland

PRESENTED BY

Mr Bhailalbhai C. Patel

[*Extracts from the Presentation by Mr B. C. Patel from Livingston, Scotland at the 1974 Annual Conference of the American Society of Planning Officials in Chicago, USA.*]

★ ★ ★

LIVINGSTON is Scotland's fourth New Town. Unlike other new towns, Livingston is the first new town being developed with a regional concept ....

It is located between Edinburgh and Glasgow, on the main communication network (M8), 15 miles to the west of Edinburgh and 35 miles east of Glasgow, which forms the northern boundary of Livingston. The M8 is connected with the main roads system of the new town. The M8 will eventually be linked with the national road network via M74 to the south, and the M9 and M90 to the north (Scottish Highlands). The most suitable physical location has played a major part in the selection of the site for Livingston and the centre for a growth area.

Airport connections are first class, as Edinburgh Airport is only within 15 minutes drive from Livingston and only one hour flying time from London. Edinburgh is already being developed as an international airport.

Seaports of Leith and Grangemouth lie on the river Forth only 15 miles north and east of Livingston New Town. Clyde ports on the west, including a major container terminal at Greenock, are 40 miles from the new town. All these are easily accessible from Livingston by high standard road system.

Two railway lines cross the designated area. A railway station is being planned and will be available to Livingston people in the very near future.

Livingston is within easy reach of a number of universities, thus providing a first class facility for higher education, and proves attractive to the science-based industries, which will play an important role in Scotland's economic growth.

Lothian's Regional Plan

After designating the site for Livingston New Town, the Secretary of State for Scotland commissioned the late Professor Robert Matthews of Edinburgh University and the late J O Robertson of Glasgow University to prepare a comprehensive physical and socio-economic survey and Plan covering an area of 80 square miles around the new town area ....

The New Town site occupies an area within which there are three existing communities of Livingston Village, Livingston Station (now Deans) and Bellsquarry. There are also several other villages closely situated (located) around Livingston. So Livingston is going to be the throbbing heart of all these communities forming an area called 'Greater Livingston Growth Area'.

The main purpose of developing a new town in the Lothians is to provide housing, employment and all other facilities of life in a pleasant environment for the people who like to come to this new community and settle.

Before Livingston was designated in 1962, the area itself was largely agricultural land, but a labour force of some 30,000 was employed in the rest of the Growth Area. A large proportion of this was employed in the declining mining industries. Thus there existed a potential labour force in the area ....

It was recommended that expansion in the new town should be related to defined groups of towns and villages close to the designated area. These are Bathgate, Armadale, Whitburn, Blackburn, Polbeth and West Calder to the west of the area having large industrial developments. Another group is Broxburn, Uphall, Winchburgh and Pumpherston, suitable for residential as well as industrial development. The third group is Mid Calder, East Calder and Oakbank with a potential for substantial residential expansion.

The most important recommendation of the plan for Livingston itself was to create a regional centre, containing major shopping facilities, office accommodation, educational and recreational facilities, a regional bus depot, parking facilities and hotel accommodation to serve the whole of the growth area.

For recreation the plan proposed a linear park along the Valley of Almond River which runs through the area. It also proposed country parks among the Bathgate hills to the north and the Pentland Hills in the south. The plan also proposed a rehabilitation programme for derelict areas and particularly of large oil shale bings on the east side of the designated site. This was considered to be of the utmost priority so that the developments in the area could take place in pleasant surroundings without reminders of industrial decline ….

Proposals

First of all it is appropriate to say that Livingston is the third generation new town since the initiation of the new town concept in 1946 in the United Kingdom. The fundamental principles are:

1 To develop a modern town taking into account its regional and national function;
2 It is expected that a large proportion of the population will immigrate from Glasgow's overspill and west of Scotland.
3 Creation of Livingston New Town would aid the regional and national economic expansion.
4 Good accessibility to all the facilities locally and in the region as a whole and even to neighbourhood facilities.
5 Flexibility: the plan should be flexible enough to accommodate any changes that may be required in the course of the development.
6 A safe and comfortable environment minimising inconvenience and conflict between pedestrians and vehicles.

7 Creation of a visually interesting environment with a clearly defined pattern of land use.

8 Freedom from pollution, noise and exposure to inclement weather.

9 Social needs of the new community to be planned and catered for.

10 Community facilities should be provided to match the build-up of population.

11 There should be public participation in the creation of Livingston as far as possible.

12 The population should be balanced in terms of age and income groups.

13 The investment should be cost effective giving good value for money.

14 The town must develop a healthy economy and become self-supporting ....

★　★　★

Now I am going to say something about the people. As explained earlier, a major proportion of the population was to come from Glasgow and the west of Scotland. It is attempted to establish a social balance by attracting people from all age groups – *ie* younger age group, middle age group and also some elderly. The bulk of the population initially will be young married couples.

It is also attempted to create a socio-economically balanced community, attracting people of mixed income groups and also mixing them in the residential districts.

The population increase is matched with the growth in employment opportunities as far as possible. The principal employment is in the manufacturing and service industries ....

Finally, I am going to talk about a very interesting social and community development project. It is called 'Lanthorn' .... The complex is situated between the two housing areas in Dedridge district which I was responsible for designing and implementation of housing developments. So indirectly I was involved in the development of Lanthorn, relating its location with the surrounding housing areas. I was also involved in the preparation of the planning proposals for the Dedridge district as a whole. 'Lanthorn' is an old Scots word meaning light and warmth. Lanthorn is the result of experience in social and community development in the earlier districts of the town. Lanthorn should be thought of not only as a building, but also as a dialogue between people and the agencies who volunteer to serve it.

It will offer genuine possibilities for self-programming and decision-making by the people themselves and will give an opportunity to identify social, cultural and other needs of the community, thus achieving some measure of fulfilment. Livingston Ecumenical · Experiment, the Roman Catholic Church, Midlothian County Council's Education Department, Livingston Development Corporation and the Scottish Education Department, have taken part in the creation of this unique concept in community development. Many other individuals and community leaders have also participated in its development.

APPENDIX 2

Iona Community Prayers
for Peace and Justice

FROM
The Iona Community Worship Book

MONDAY:
Those who work for Peace and Justice –
those in the peace movement
those concerned with racial or sexual or social discrimination
prisoners of conscience

> Collect: *Peace between neighbours*
> *Peace between kindred*
> *Peace between lovers*
> *In love of the king of life.*

TUESDAY:
Those who work for Healing –
bridge builders
environmentalists, and those who work on the land
broken families and communities

> Collect: *O my soul's healer, keep me at evening*
> *Keep me at morning, keep me at noon,*
> *I am tired, astray and stumbling,*
> *Shield me from sin.*

WEDNESDAY:
Those who work for a more just Economic Order –
workers and management in industry
those who are unemployed
those whose labour is exploited

Collect: *Bless to us O God the earth beneath our feet*
Bless to us O God the path whereon we go
Bless to us O God the thing of our desire
Evermore of evermore, bless to us our rest.

THURSDAY:

Those who are engaged in Public Service –
local and national politicians, the United Nations
any involved in the processes of law
all who care for others in the home
any whose rights are denied

Collect: *My Christ, my shield, my encircler*
Each day, each night, each light, each dark,
Be near me, uphold me, my·treasure, my triumph.

FRIDAY:

Those who help us to celebrate –
artists, musicians, writers, children, friends –
the Unity of the Church

Collect: *God to enfold us, God to surround us*
God in our speaking, God in our thinking
God in our life, God in our lips
God in our souls, God in our hearts.

SATURDAY:

Prophets and Pioneers –
migrant workers,
refugees,
travellers,
our own inward journey,
and commitment to peace and justice.

Collect: *As you were before us at our life's beginning*
Be you so again at our journey's end,
As you were beside us at our soul's shaping
God be also at our journey's close.

APPENDIX 3

Bibliography

Beeson, Trevor: 'The Ministry in New Areas' in 'A Prism Pamphlet' (11) (London).

Bonhoeffer, Dietrich: *Letters and Papers from Prison* (London: SCM Press, 1971), enlarged edition.

Brandt Report – Danus Skene (with Introduction by Robin Barbour) (Edinburgh: SCAWD).

Church and the Disorder of Society, The (London: SCM Press, 1948).

'Come Holy Spirit, Renew the Whole Creation', one of six Bible Studies prepared for the Seventh Assembly of the World Council of Churches in Canberra.

Ecumenical Review, The (Geneva: World Council of Churches publications), quarterly publication.

Iona Community Worship Book (early edition, published by The Iona Community, no date).

Keenan, Brian: *An Evil Cradling.*

King, Coretta Scott: *My Life with Martin Luther King* (Hodder & Stoughton, 1970).

Moltmann, Jürgen: *The Open Church* (London: SCM Press, 1978).

Newbigin, Lesslie: *The Household of God* (1952).

Newbigin, Lesslie: *The Open Secret* (London: SPCK, 1978).

Newbigin, Lesslie: *Unfinished Agenda* (Edinburgh: Saint Andrew Press, 1994).

Oxford Book of Prayers, The (Oxford: Oxford University Press).

Rosen, McKinney and Carroll: *Varieties of Religious Presence* (New York: The Pilgrim Press).

Smith, Peter (ed): *The Caring Church* (Derby: Peter Smith Ltd, 1964).

Vannier, Jean: *Man and Woman He made them* (London: Darton, Longman & Todd).

Vannier, Jean: *Community and Growth.*

Wickam, E.R.: *Church and People in an Industrial City* (London: Lutterworth Press).

William Templeton Foundation: A Series of Occasional Papers (Manchester: Manchester Business School).

'With All God's People' in the Ecumenical Prayer Cycle (Geneva: World Council of Churches publications).

The Risk Book Series (Geneva: World Council of Churches publications), especially:

Bluck, John: *Everyday Ecumenism* (no. 35).

Castro, Emilio: *When We Pray Together* (no. 40).

Fung, Raymond: *The Isaiah Vision* (no. 52).

Granberg-Michaelson, Karin: *Healing Community* (no. 150).

Granberg-Michaelson, Wesley: *Redeeming the Creation* (no. 55).

Hinton, Jeanne: *Walking in the Same Direction* (no. 67).

Thorogood, Bernard: *One Wind, Many Flames* (no. 48).

Van Elderen, Martin: *Introducing the World Council of Churches* (no. 46).

Watley, William: *Singing the Lord's Song in a Strange Land* (no. 57).

[The World Council of Churches can be contacted at WCC, 150 route de Ferney, 1211 Geneva 20, Switzerland.]